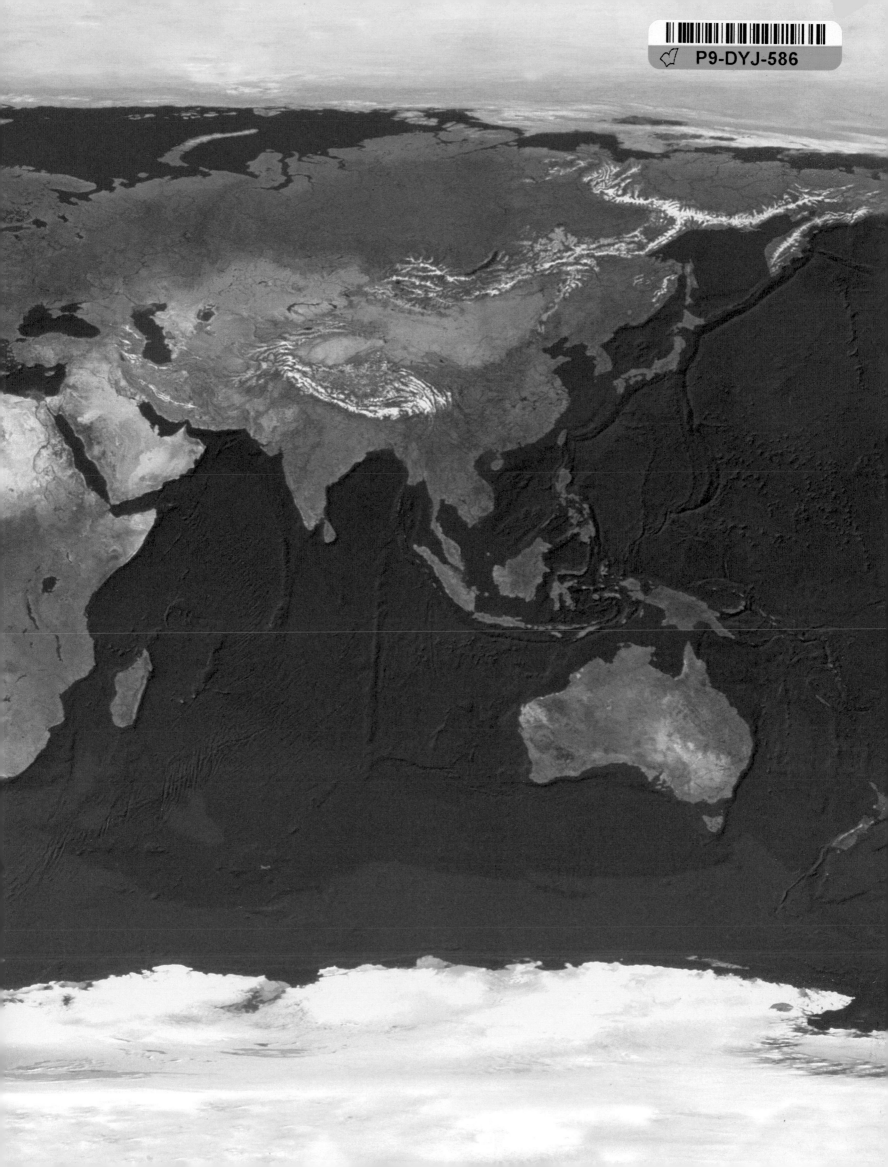

SPIRIT OF THE
POLAR
REGIONS

First published by Parragon in 2007

Parragon

Queen Street House

4 Queen Street

Bath BA1 1HE, UK

Designed, produced and packaged by Stonecastle Graphics Limited

Text by Gerard Cheshire

Edited by Philip de Ste. Croix

Designed by Sue Pressley and Paul Turner

ISBN 978-1-4054-8670-5

Printed in China

SPIRIT OF THE
POLAR
REGIONS

GERARD CHESHIRE

Bath · New York · Singapore · Hong Kong · Cologne · Delhi · Melbourne

CONTENTS

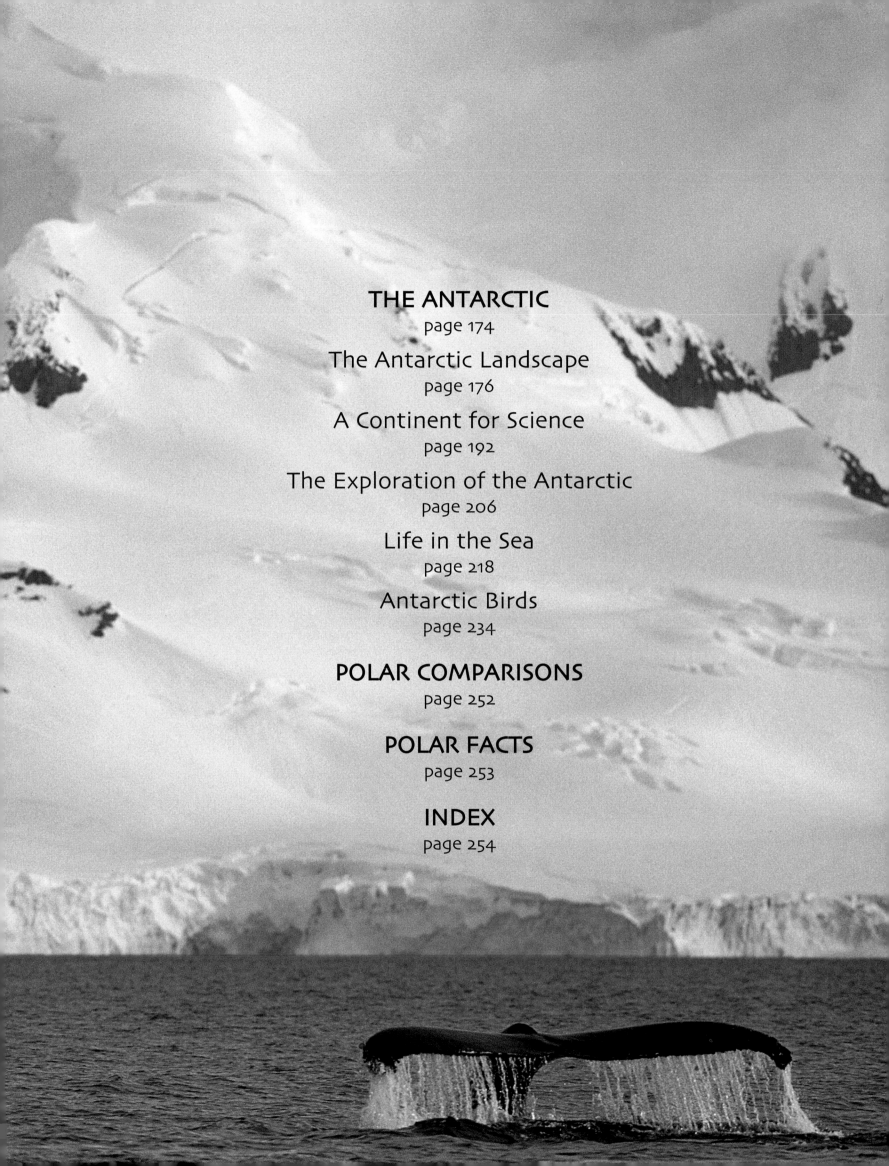

THE POLAR REGIONS

To appreciate fully the environments that make up the two polar regions it is necessary to understand the geometry and physics of the Earth's motion and orbit around the Sun. The poles of the Earth are the points that mark its axis of rotation. The line of axis is tilted 23° 26′ away from perpendicular relative to the Earth's plane of orbit around the Sun. This orbital tilt means that the amount of sunlight that reaches the polar regions during the course of a year varies significantly. This 'temporal rhythm' is defined by four distinct seasonal periods.

There are three months of almost constant darkness (the polar winter) and another three months of almost constant daylight (the polar summer). Separating summer and winter are two more three-month periods which see the transition from darkness to daylight (the polar spring) and from daylight back to darkness (the polar fall).

Of course, these seasons occur at different times of the year in the northern and southern polar regions because their temporal rhythms are six months out of alignment – midsummer's day at one pole always corresponds exactly with midwinter's day at the other, and vice versa.

The polar regions – the Arctic and Antarctic – are defined geographically by imaginary lines that circumscribe the globe, called the Arctic circle and the Antarctic circle. They lie at latitudes 66° 34′ above and below the equator respectively. This angle of latitude plus the angle of the Earth's tilt add up to 90°. This means that both circles line up precisely with the 'top' and 'bottom' of the planet in relation to the position of the Sun. In other words, only the regions inside the circles can experience 24 hours of sunlight on midsummer's day and 24 hours of darkness on midwinter's day.

Although the polar regions receive as much daylight over a whole year as any other part of the planet, they do not receive as much solar radiation. This is because the rays of the Sun have to penetrate down through the atmosphere at an oblique angle to reach the areas lying within the Arctic and Antarctic circles. In effect this makes the atmosphere thicker to penetrate with the result that much of the solar energy is absorbed by the atmosphere and never reaches the ground. The reason for this is that the particles of light that make up sunlight (also known as electromagnetic or solar radiation) have to find their way through a larger number of air molecules. This increases the chance of each light particle colliding with a molecule of air and so using up its energy before reaching the surface of the Earth.

The cumulative effect of this is to deprive the polar regions of solar energy so that they experience lower average temperatures than other parts of the world. The only other places that typically

The Arctic

Previous page: This is part of an iceberg off the coast of Antarctica. Ice is subject to weathering and erosion just like the rock faces that make up more familiar coastlines. The elements of wind, rain, sunshine, and waves have slowly eaten away the ice until a section has fallen away to leave an arch.

exhibit near-freezing or sub-zero temperatures are those at the highest altitudes (mountain peaks) and those at the lowest altitudes (ocean trenches) as they also receive little or no solar radiation.

This reduced level of solar radiation means that there is relatively little energy available to warm gases, liquids, or solids. This results in frozen environments where air, land, and sea temperatures seldom rise much above 32°F (0°C).

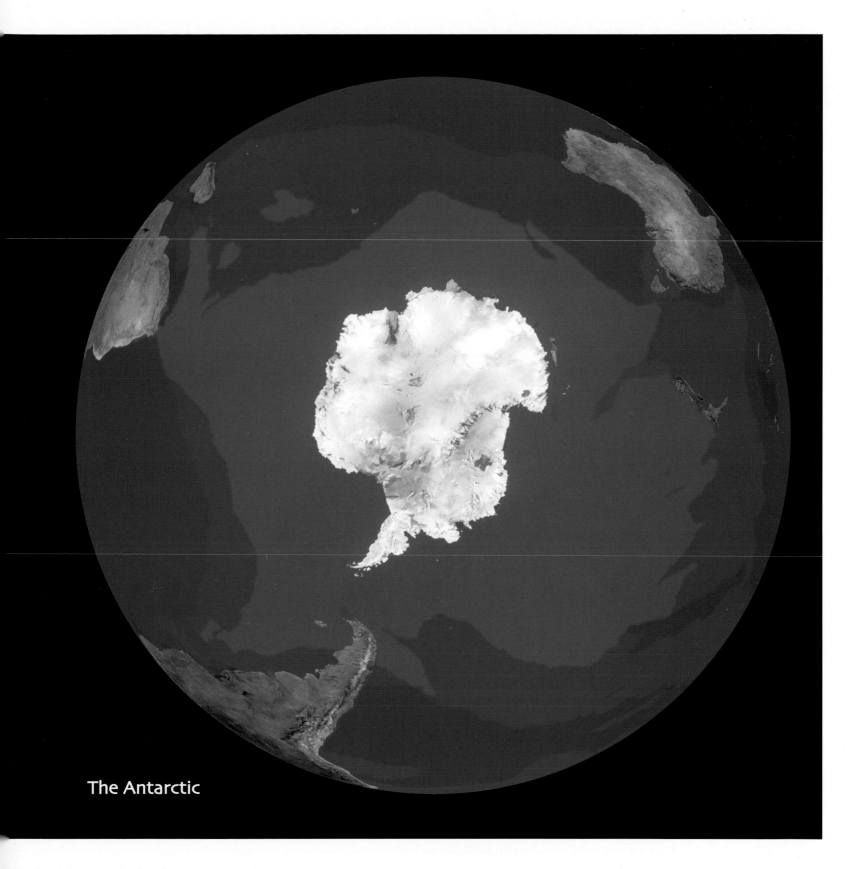

The Antarctic

The polar regions are therefore habitats which display characteristics peculiar to themselves, and polar animals and plants come equipped with many evolved adaptations and strategies that enable them to eke out their living in conditions that species from warmer climes would undoubtedly find too extreme to survive. We shall discover much more about them in the course of this book.

Above and opposite: These images show the Arctic region (left) and Antarctic region (right) from a perspective that might be obtained from space while positioned exactly above each pole. The white ice of the Arctic is largely floating on the Arctic Ocean, while that of the Antarctic is centered on the landmass of Antarctica.

Above: During the height of summer in the Arctic and Antarctic the Sun fails to set. This image is actually a series of superimposed time-lapsed photographs that show how the Sun skirts across the horizon without actually vanishing from view. The result is continual daylight and an absence of night.

Right: Mount Erebus is located on Ross Island, Antarctica. It is the most southerly active volcano on Earth. It was erupting at the time of its discovery by James Clark Ross in 1841. It has three sister volcanoes which are all inactive. Erebus is the name of the son of the god of chaos in Greek myth and hence the personification of darkness.

Above: This is part of Greenland known as Disko Bay. Legend has it that Eric the Red, a Norwegian adventurer, founded the first Nordic settlement at the bay, where trade was done with the Inuit people. By the 15th century a shift in temperature made the bay inaccessible due to the presence of year-round ice.

Left: These are snow-covered mountains in a northerly region of Sweden known as Lapland. They bear more than a passing resemblance to the frozen ranges in Antarctica, such is the general similarity between the landscapes of the polar regions.

Previous pages: This is a typical scene showing the 'treeline,' where conifer forest gives way to the alpine zone on a mountainside due to altitude. This particular image was photographed in Alaska, but the same transition can be seen in many subpolar mountain ranges in both the northern and southern hemispheres.

Above: This is a phenomenon known as 'dirty ice.' It is a telltale sign that the ice originates from a glacier, as the dirt usually consists of particles of rock that have been hewn from the substrate by the glacier as it has traveled down toward the shoreline. The material is eventually dropped to form what is known as a moraine deposit.

Above: Icebergs are sections of glaciers that have broken off and floated out to sea. Over time they melt away in a characteristic manner. The submerged ice tends to diminish until the iceberg becomes top heavy. It then rotates to accommodate its new center of gravity and the process is repeated.

Right: This ice cliff looks as though it might have been sculpted by human hand. In fact it has been eroded by tides and crosswinds, resulting in a terraced appearance. Several chunks have fallen away because the integrity of the supporting ice below has been lost.

Right: These immense ice cliffs in Antarctica have not been in existence for a long enough time to be eroded by the elements. Instead they are like pristine rock faces, newly exposed by the breaking away of sections – a process known as calving. Deep vertical cracks indicate that new calving incidents are imminent.

THE ARCTIC

*T*o the uninitiated, the Arctic and Antarctic look essentially similar to one another – they seem uniformly white, bleak, and frozen. In fact, this is a misapprehension. Quite large areas of North America, Europe and Asia extend into the Arctic circle, whereas only the continent of Antarctica itself can be found in the Antarctic circle. This means that a far greater diversity of terrestrial habitats are found in the northern latitudes and this, in turn, means that the Arctic plays host to a greater number and range of land-living animals than the Antarctic. Chief among them is the top predator of the Arctic region – the polar bear.

This magnificent hunter has no counterpart in the Antarctic.

For similar reasons of geography, several indigenous human populations

have settled in the countries that ring the Arctic and developed their

characteristic cultures, whereas the human presence on Antarctica is

limited to a handful of adventurous tourists and a scientific community

that depends on an external supply line for vital stores and support.

Plant life too varies significantly. The Arctic supports trees

and tundra; plant life on Antarctica consists mainly of mosses,

liverworts and lichens.

THE ARCTIC LANDSCAPE

Unlike the Antarctic, which contains its own continent of Antarctica, there is no Arctic continent or landmass – nothing that we might call 'Arctica.' Instead there is only the Arctic Ocean which is bounded, in a roughly circular manner, by the northernmost coasts and islands of the three continents of North America, Europe, and Asia.

Politically the countries with Arctic coastline are Canada, Denmark (Greenland), Norway, Russia and the USA (Alaska). In addition, Sweden and Finland have Arctic territory but no coastline, while Iceland lies just outside the Arctic circle with only a few northerly islands comprising a tiny amount of Arctic territory.

It may come as something of a surprise to learn that the Arctic circle does not have a fixed latitude, but drifts northward and southward over time, as does the Antarctic circle. This is because the Earth 'nutates' which means that it oscillates or wobbles on its axis. It has a short-term nutation period of 18.6 years during which time its tilt oscillates over about 9′ (0.15°) which corresponds to a 919ft (280m) shift on the surface, or 49ft (15m) per year. Its long-term nutation spans 41,000 years with a range of about 41′ (0.68°), corresponding to 47 miles (76km) or 6ft (1.85m) per year.

Although these nutational shifts may seem quite insignificant, they still have an effect on the amount of solar radiation that is absorbed by the Earth. Currently the polar regions are decreasing in size, because the axis is straightening up. This means that the Earth's surface is being subjected to rising levels of solar radiation, which undoubtedly plays its part in the phenomenon of global warming.

Other factors in the equation are perturbations in the actual orbit of the Earth around the Sun. Due to the gravitational pull of the other planets, the Earth's orbital path gyrates like a hula-hoop around the waist of a gymnast. This makes the orbit oscillate between circular and elliptical shapes, so that the Earth's distance from the Sun varies.

There is also a difference between the geographic North Pole and the magnetic North Pole. Scientists have concluded that there must be a solid iron-rich core to the Earth that rotates within a fluid layer that lies beneath the Earth's crust. In effect, it works like a giant dynamo or motor so that the Earth generates its own electromagnetic field. However, compass readings of the field indicate clearly that the axis of the core's rotation is not exactly aligned with the axis of the globe itself.

Furthermore it also wobbles (nutates) but in a far more dramatic fashion. The north and south magnetic poles have drifted by over 12° latitude and 15° longitude since the early 19th century. In that time their movements have accelerated from

Above: In some parts of the world dirty ice in glaciers is caused by their proximity to active volcanoes. The fallout from volcanic eruptions is known as pyroclastic material. It varies in particle size from fine ash to chunks of lava that have solidified while traveling through the air.

Previous page: Due to the altitude in the mountains precipitation always falls as snow rather than rain. That means that glaciers are continually fed with new layers of snow, which gradually compact into ice. Glaciers can be thought of as perpetual conveyor belts of ice, running down from the mountain peaks to the foothills.

around 6 miles (10km) to 25 miles (40km) per year. Geologists have also established by studying the magnetic alignments of igneous rocks that the magnetic poles have always shifted greatly and sometimes the Earth's magnetic polarity has even switched over entirely in the history of the planet.

Certainly the nutational movements of both the inner and outer spheres of the Earth must influence one another in certain ways, although so far this phenomenon is not fully understood. Nevertheless, in turn they must have had an influence in determining the continual alterations recorded in the Arctic and Antarctic circles. When working in sympathy with one another they may cause each of the polar regions to expand or contract by as much as 580,000 sq miles (1.5 million km^2). That equates to an area roughly the size of western Europe being lost or gained to the polar regions, albeit over the course of tens of thousands of years. This waxing and waning of the polar regions represents a significant shift in the Earth's ability to absorb solar radiation at its surface over geological time. We have the ice ages (glacials) and warm ages (interglacials) as proof of that.

Left: Iceland is a good example of an actively volcanic polar region. Inevitably glaciers become absolutely filthy with ash, which stains the ice and snow to tones of gray and even black. Glaciers move slowly too, which gives them plenty of time to become adulterated and discolored by airborne debris.

Following pages: Volcanic activity can result in the release of spectacular jets of water known as geysers. Fissures in the Earth's crust allow water to drain down to regions where the rock is very hot. This water then reaches boiling point and the expanding steam results in a fountain of hot water being forced skyward.

Left: When volcanoes cease to be active their craters inevitably fill up with rain water and snow to form volcanic lakes. These lakes can sit for long periods of time, until any dissolved gases have escaped. If they then freeze, they form 'blue ice' containing chemical deposits which can be useful to scientists for analysis.

Opposite: This is a rare event known as a sub-glacier eruption, where a volcano has erupted through its side and exploded a glacier in the process. The result is a pall of smoke and ash together with vaporized ice (steam) rising high into the sky. A consequence of this eruption will be that any rainfall will be polluted by the volcanic debris thrown into the air.

Below: In places where the rocks are heated due to volcanic activity, the phenomenon is described as geothermal. This picture shows a hot spring in Iceland. The colors are due to deposits of minerals dissolved in the water and brought to the surface, where specialized bacteria also flourish.

CLIMATIC CONDITIONS

Sub-zero temperatures inevitably promote the formation of ice, which dominates both the landscape and seascape of the Arctic more-or-less all year round.

The Arctic Ocean has a perpetual and vast floating ice 'continent' at its center, which grows and diminishes in size with the passing of the Arctic winters and summers. It constantly moves about due to convection currents in the waters below and winds in the air above.

At its edges the ice breaks away into floes that migrate into open water where they become temporary islands. These are joined by icebergs, which are the offspring of the many glaciers that reach the sea at the Arctic coastline having inched their way for hundreds or thousands of years down from inland valleys.

Some islands and coasts are perpetually encrusted with ice sheets – particularly Greenland and others that lie nearest to the geographic North Pole – and they never experience enough solar energy for the ice to melt away. In other parts the covering of ice and snow melts away during the Arctic spring and summer so

Top: This photograph illustrates clearly how glaciers are created over long passages of time. The staining of the ice betrays strata that have been laid down over centuries.

Right: This glacier terminates on land rather than flowing into the sea. This is seen as a sign of global warming in many places, as the noses of glaciers are known to be retreating with each passing year.

that the ground is briefly but periodically freed from its frozen straitjacket. Nevertheless, just a few inches below the surface the ground remains frozen solid. This is known as the permanent frost or permafrost.

When it comes to the enduring battle between freezing and thawing in the Arctic region, a definite 'seesaw' effect can be observed both on land and out to sea. Ice and snow are very reflective surfaces, so they don't readily absorb solar radiation. This means that it takes a long time for sunshine to begin to have a defrosting effect. In fact, it only really begins to take effect once the air molecules start to warm up, and their contact with the ice transfers sufficient energy for thawing to take place.

However, once it begins then there is a significant acceleration in the rate of thawing – hence the 'seesawing.' This occurs because the exposed ocean and land surfaces are generally non-reflective of solar radiation, and hence they absorb energy and warm up. With warm air circulating above and warm water or land beneath, the ice melts increasingly rapidly.

Conversely, the absorbed energy is quickly lost to the air and carried away once levels of solar radiation begin to fall in the fall months. This is because neither the ocean nor the land can actually store very much heat energy during the warmer months. Only the upper levels of the ocean waters manage to climb just above freezing point. The land can warm up much more than the sea, but again only in a very thin substrate layer lying above the permafrost is affected.

Scientists recognize that glacial periods can come upon the Earth very quickly because it only takes a few cold summers for snow and ice to accumulate sufficiently to tip the climatic balance. This can occur after only a slight fall in annual temperatures, that may be caused by a large volcanic eruption throwing huge quantities of dust into the atmosphere.

Aside from sunlight, the only other significant sources of ambient energy are volcanic activity and oceanic drift. Iceland is formed entirely from igneous rock spewed up from submarine volcanoes. It lies on a fault line between two of the Earth's tectonic plates, and subterranean movements allow molten rock (magma) to leak out from the Earth's crust. It still exhibits

Left: An aerial view of an enormous 'U'-shaped glacial valley in Alaska. Several minor glaciers feed into the main glacier to form hanging valleys along the sides.

volcanic activity today, including hot springs and geysers that are created by water flowing below ground and becoming heated.

Both the Pacific and Atlantic oceans contain circulating currents of water known as drifts. In the case of the Pacific Ocean, there is only a small gateway – the Bering strait – into the Arctic Ocean, but the Atlantic Ocean flows into the Arctic Ocean at a far wider point – the Norwegian sea – and it carries with it warmth from equatorial waters flowing northward.

Although both poles experience the same levels of solar radiation each year, there is a marked difference in their overall climates. This has to do with a number of influencing factors – not least their proximity to landmasses.

Most of the Arctic coastline belongs to the continents of North America and Asia. Both are huge landmasses that extend southward as far as the sub-equatorial zone. Air currents circulating over them get warmed up and then flow northward where they provide warming energy to the Arctic. This has a significant effect on environmental conditions throughout the territory within the Arctic circle.

The only landmass with a truly polar climate is Greenland. This is because it is a large island surrounded by ocean. Inland regions of Greenland remain at sub-zero temperatures throughout the year, ranging from about minus 25°F (-5°C) in the summer to minus 31°F (-35°C) in the winter. Consequently, it never rains in Greenland, it only snows, just as it does over the ice continent surrounding the North Pole itself.

At its eastern, western, and southern coasts Greenland shares its climate with the northern coastal regions of North America and Asia. This is known as the tundra climate. In these areas the land generally thaws in spring and summer so that it rains for a few months. Liquid water means that these places can support plant and animal life much more readily than the polar habitats. Temperatures in tundra regions range from about 68°F(20°C) in the summer to minus 4°F (-20°C) in the winter.

Forming an irregular strip just below the tundra region, and straddling the Arctic circle, is the transitional zone, marking the divide between tundra and temperate climates. Here freezing temperatures typically occur only at the height of winter, and plants and animals can inhabit far more congenial habitats. Levels of rainfall and snowfall tend to be higher year round in the transitional zone and temperatures range from 77°F (25°C) in summer to minus 14°F (-10°C) in winter.

In Alaska and Norway there are also mountain ranges that provide alpine climates. In essence these are much like the tundra

habitats except that they remain frozen, due to their altitude, during the summer months when the surrounding terrain has defrosted.

The whole of the Arctic region can experience very strong winds and blizzards, especially in the wintertime. The reason for this is that convection currents are created between zones of cold air to the north and warm air to the south. Extremes in air temperature lead to extremes in air pressure, and the cold air sinks below the warm air with such energy that gale force winds are generated. The famous 'north winds' are caused by those cold air fronts rushing southward to make way for warm air fronts pushing down from above.

Above: This exposed face contains some of the oldest known types of rock on the planet. The formation, found in Greenland, is known as the Isua Greenstone Belt. Greenstone is a mix of sedimentary and volcanic rock about 3.8 billion years old, which may harbor clues about the origins of life.

Left: Despite its apparent inhospitableness, this landscape is home-sweet-home to the polar bear. It is equipped with extremely powerful legs with robust feet and claws that enable it to clamber about on icy surfaces that would not be negotiable by a human, even one equipped with ice boots and picks.

Previous pages: The ice of glaciers is subjected to forces as it moves along. The result can be odd-looking formations, where the ice splits and breaks up as the glacier twists and bends over the rock beneath.

Below: Calving is the name given to the process where chunks of ice break away from the nose of a glacier. This is because it happens suddenly rather like newborn calves falling from their mothers.

Above: The difference between icebergs and ice floes is that the former originate in glaciers, like those seen in this picture. The latter are flatter pieces of ice that break off from areas of pack ice which forms on the surface of the water.

Right: The Vatnajökull glacier in Iceland is a giant among glaciers, occupying more than 8 percent of the country. At its terminal end – part of which is seen here – it is an incredible 80 miles (130km) wide. In addition to this the ice is an average of 875yd (800m) thick.

Above: Sometimes natural ice formations can possess sculptural qualities reminiscent of the work of modernist sculptors. Here a block of ice in a glacial lake looks as though it could be an enormous abstract reclining figure carved from plaster of Paris, ready to be cast in bronze.

Right: This photograph shows how freshwater can remain frozen solid in the presence of fluid seawater. The reason is that the salt in the seawater lowers its freezing point below zero. In addition, the kinetic energy generated by the movement of the waves provides a certain amount of warmth.

Above: This is the seed head of Arctic cotton-grass, which is actually a type of sedge rather than a grass. Each seed comes equipped with cotton-like plumes. These enable the seeds to travel through the air and they even allow them to skit across open water.

Left: Springtime in Arctic Alaska brings a flush of color as flowering plants hurry about their business of blooming to attract insects for the purpose of fertilization. This scene is dominated by the cerise flowers of an Arctic vetch known as liquorice root.

Following pages: Here in the Yukon, Canada, the fall colors of the Arctic are every bit as striking as those of the springtime flowers. Before long they will be lost beneath a blanket of fresh snow.

THE NORTHERN LIGHTS

At certain times of the year a beautiful phenomenon known as the aurora borealis or northern lights can be seen in the skies above the Arctic region. The same phenomenon occurs in the Antarctic region, where it is known as the aurora australis or southern lights. Auroras are caused by interaction between charged particles that flow out from the Sun and atoms in the upper atmosphere. When the particles and atoms collide, energy is released in the form of light. Countless billions of these collisions result in dramatic, multicolored light displays in the night sky. The colors are predominantly reds and greens but changing wavelengths can produce a kaleidoscopic effect with blues, yellows, and whites also in evidence.

The reason that they occur at the polar regions is that the solar radiation, or the solar wind as it is known scientifically, is funneled toward the magnetic poles by electromagnetic attraction, so that the charged particles become highly concentrated in these areas. Consequently an aurora typically takes the form of an arch, or horseshoe, shape with its apex drawn toward the magnetic pole. The display of light itself can take many shapes, such as arcs, bands, coronas, curtains, and rays, which move about with remarkable speed and beauty.

Right: The light displays of aurorae move about in the sky with great rapidity. This is because the photons from the Sun are traveling at the speed of light, so waves of them can move from one place to another in an instant, where they then interact with charged particles and release light.

LIFE IN THE ARCTIC

Animals that live in the Arctic employ a number of strategies to assist in their survival. Some species are active only during the warmer months and go into hibernation when the weather turns harsh. Others partially hibernate by punctuating their dormancy with periods of activity. Still others migrate between the Arctic and warmer territories farther south, while the remainder stay active as Arctic residents.

SURVIVAL STRATEGIES

Those animals that struggle to find sufficient food during the Arctic winter, and are unable to fly, swim, or walk to more temperate climes, find that the most sensible strategy is to hide away in a state of suspended animation or 'hibernation' (the word is derived from 'hibernare' the Latin for 'to winter').

Hibernating animals slow down their metabolisms to conserve their energy supplies. Their body temperatures drop to just above freezing and their heart rates fall dramatically to only a few beats per minute. To hibernate successfully these animals need to fatten themselves up when food is plentiful in late summer. Their subcutaneous fat is their sole source of energy and nutrition until the habitat begins to warm up in the springtime. This means that it is important that they have very effective insulation in the form of fur, an ample fat layer, and a good nest and warm bedding that is protected from the elements. More often than not, hibernation takes place in the safety of burrows or between crevices in rocks.

Some animals do their best to fatten themselves up for hibernation but still need to supplement their energy supplies over winter with more food. To achieve partial hibernation they have to be able to fall into and rouse themselves out of the dormant state when necessary. Some species create their nests and dens in places where it is easy to make quick foraging expeditions during any break in the severest weather. Storing foodstuffs in caches before the onset of winter is also a very useful ploy, enabling animals to top up their energy reserves at leisure and in the comfort of their winter quarters.

For many animals the most logical strategy when the weather turns cold is to move out for the duration, hence the term 'migrate' from the Latin 'migrare' meaning to move or shift. Whether airborne, waterborne, or landborne, animals migrate in their droves to warmer places.

Some species move only a little farther south to escape the worst of the Arctic winter weather, while others travel considerable distances to far-off lands. Migratory distances are chiefly dictated by the diets of the migrating animals. Equally, the

Previous page: Polar bears are well adapted to Arctic life. They have low surface-area-to-volume ratio to conserve body heat. They have large paws for treading snow and their fur provides camouflage.

Right: Snow geese, like many other migratory birds, fly in 'V'-shaped formations called skeins. Low pressure points created by the wings of the bird in front provide an advantage to the bird behind.

Arctic region has to offer a considerable incentive for them to return each year. This incentive is a glut of food sufficient to support them and their offspring during the breeding season.

Some animals don't need to hibernate or migrate, although they do find it sensible to avoid or shelter from the very worst of the Arctic winter weather. These are the larger animals, which are capable of finding enough food regularly to satisfy their survival requirements. In fact, the indigenous human populations of the Arctic may be counted among this group. When originally discovered they were living in as near to a 'wild' or 'natural' condition as any other native population on the planet. Indeed, their material culture – their weapons, tools, and clothing – was entirely derived from parts of the animals they hunted.

BREEDING STRATEGIES

For all plants and animals of the Arctic, successful reproduction is all about careful timing. For smaller mammals, birds, reptiles, and amphibians there is only a brief window of opportunity in the shape of a short-lived Arctic summer. As soon as the weather becomes milder in late spring, they quickly have to get on with the business of establishing territories, finding mates, and breeding so that offspring are born in time to take advantage of the summer's seasonal glut of food. Similarly, plants need to flower and be fertilized in order to produce their seed.

The aim of both animals and plants is to complete their reproductive cycles before the onset of the fall, so that their offspring can disperse or disseminate as the new generation.

The diets of animals are often more complex than the terms carnivore, herbivore, and omnivore suggest and the availability of foodstuffs during the brief breeding season varies for each species. For example, there are animals that specialize in eating insects, spiders, and other invertebrates, while others specialize in eating seeds, fruits, or nuts. Some insects specialize in eating

nectar, others eat leaves and there are those that suck sap or eat wood. Other specialist feeders only eat roots or grasses or fungi.

Most animals described as carnivores or herbivores are actually omnivorous to a certain extent – if they were not, then they would fail to take in an appropriate variety of nutrients and vitamins. Consequently, carnivores instinctively supplement their diets with vegetable matter from time to time, and herbivores do it incidentally by consuming invertebrates with their foliage.

The larger mammals of the Arctic, although still constrained by the seasons, need to employ a slightly different strategy with regard to reproduction. The larger a mammal species is, then the longer its gestation period will generally be. This means that large mammals have no option but to mate during the fall or winter months to ensure that the birth will coincide with the following springtime. In this way they give their offspring the best chance of developing sufficiently over the summer months to survive the following winter.

The single biggest problem faced by plants in the Arctic is a general lack of liquid water (as opposed to snow and ice). They need flowing water for their vascular systems to function, enabling them to feed, grow, and reproduce.

Above: Female polar bears give birth to their offspring while holed up in ice caves during the winter months. This ensures that the cubs can take full advantage of the spring and summer months' glut of food.

Left: Young seals are gorged on milk that is the richest in nutrients among mammals. This enables the pups to grow quickly and put on thick layers of blubber as protection from the winter temperatures.

Many herbaceous plants, along with ferns and fungi, simply have to wait until the springtime thaw before they can burst into life, whether from spores, seed, or root stock. They then make the most of the summer warmth to complete their lifecycles before dying down with the return of cold.

Annual and perennial plants tend to be low-growing in the Arctic, as this protects them from frosts and chill winds that might otherwise kill off their tender parts during the growing season.

Some plants have evolved another form of protection from the cold by producing sap which has a lower freezing point than water. Solutes are dissolved in the sap that act as antifreeze agents. This prevents the water from expanding and forming ice crystals within the plant cells, which would rupture the cell walls and destroy them.

Many woody plants have adapted to be shallow-rooting so as to take full advantage of the thin layer of substrate containing fluid water above the permafrost. Some trees are also adapted to tolerate low moisture, nutrition, and energy levels. Conifers have needle-shaped leaves to reduce their surface area and so lessen evaporation from the leaf surface. They are also evergreen which means they do not have to use precious resources to re-grow their leaves with each new year. It also guarantees that they can begin photosynthesizing very early on in the growing season and continue to do so until late in the season as well.

Above: Here a moose or elk calf is supplementing its milk diet with the flowers and shoots of a common northern plant, known as fireweed in America and rosebay willowherb in Britain.

Right: This is a species of deer known in America as the caribou, but as the reindeer in northern Europe. It is an extremely hardy animal, able to eke out a living by eating tundra plants.

Above: This purple saxifrage is a typical plant of the Arctic region. It is a ground-hugging species, never growing more than a few inches in height, but spreading to form extensive cushions of foliage. This means it remains protected from the worst weather but maximizes its exposure to sunlight.

Right: The beautiful Iceland poppy flower. This pale orange or tangerine color is the typical form, but it occasionally comes in whites, yellows, deep oranges, and reds.

Opposite: These striking yellow flowers are those of the glacier avens. The plant is remarkable for beginning to flower while snow still lies on the ground. It has dark foliage which warms in the sunlight so that the plant melts away a patch of snow. The flower buds then rise up and bloom.

Above: The leaves of many plants turn to yellows, oranges, and reds in the fall because the green chlorophyll breaks down, allowing other pigments to reveal their colors. Chlorophyll is used by plants during the growing season to convert the energy in sunlight into food by the process known as photosynthesis.

Left: There are several species of flowering plants known commonly as paintbrushes, due to the shape of the flower buds, which resemble the brushes once used by Native Americans to daub paint on their bodies. This is the elegant paintbrush, which comes in a variety of whites and pinks.

Above: Snow geese prefer to feed in flocks rather than on their own. This affords them protection against predators, such as Arctic foxes. This is partly because sentry geese sound the alarm if predators are seen nearby. In addition the noise and commotion of the flock it makes it confusing for a predator to single out a particular target.

Right: Reindeer instinctively migrate long distances over the Arctic tundra in search of food. To conserve their energy, they will often take shortcuts fraught with risk. Here a herd can be seen crossing a coastal inlet, or fjord, at low tide to save having to walk all the way round the shoreline.

Below: Sea otters are so well insulated against the cold water that they happily float about on their backs looking rather like contented holiday makers in the Caribbean. Their secret is their pelt, which has more hairs per given area than any other mammal's. This means that the water doesn't even reach the skin.

Above: Gray seals have benefited greatly over recent years from official protection. They used to be hunted for their fur and blubber, which led to a dramatic decline in their numbers on both sides of the north Atlantic. They are now recolonizing coastlines where they were once hunted virtually to extinction.

Right: Polar bears spend a great deal of their time traveling on pack ice rather than on land, although the distinction isn't necessarily that clear at times. Pack ice tends to break up into islands with smaller ice floes at the edges which the bears use as stepping stones.

Left: This is the Arctic fox in its natural habitat. Unlike the polar bear, which is big enough to prey on large marine mammals, the Arctic fox is a small animal. This means that it doesn't need to find as much food as a polar bear does to survive, but it also means that it has to specialize in eating Arctic birds and rodents.

HUMANS IN THE ARCTIC

There is some debate about the precise dating of the earliest human presence in the Americas. What is known for certain is that indigenous populations are all of Oriental or Mongoloid stock and must have arrived via the Bering strait when it was frozen over, either in wintertime or during the end of the last ice age perhaps 8500 years ago. From that point of access they then dispersed across both North and South America.

As the Americas became increasingly peopled, inevitably territories and resources were fought over. This meant that some tribes were forced out into the less hospitable areas, such as the Arctic region. Humans are remarkably adaptable, however, thanks to their ability to use materials to make tools, weapons, clothing, and housing. In fact, the indigenous populations were very successful at exploiting the Arctic environment and they had developed a complex material and social culture by the time European explorers arrived.

There are actually two indigenous peoples in the North American Arctic region – the Inuit and the Yupik – and they speak different languages. The Inuit inhabit western Greenland, northern Canada, and eastern Alaska, while the Yupik frequent north-eastern Siberia, western Alaska, and the volcanic Aleutian Islands, which lie in a chain off the Alaska peninsula, beneath the Bering sea.

They are known collectively, by anthropologists and archeologists, as Eskimos, but this term is now considered politically incorrect for general use as the populations themselves draw a racial and cultural distinction between one another. In addition, the term 'Paleo-Eskimo' is used to describe the forebears of the modern population, who colonized the Arctic in the late Stone Age. Recently the term 'Inupik' (a contraction of 'Inuit-Yupik') has been coined as a potentially acceptable alternative to 'Eskimo.'

The Inuit number about 60,000 and speak a language called Inupiaq or Inuktitut. An individual from the Inuit is known as an Inuk. The Yupik number only 3000 and speak a language of the same name. Individuals are known as Yupiks or Aleuts. Both the Inupiaq and Yupik languages belong to a linguistic group known as the Eskimo-Aleut family.

Surviving populations of Inuit and Yupik are fast becoming accustomed to the trappings of the modern world, simply because they make life more comfortable and convenient. While they still often practice the traditional skills, like hunting for seal and other Arctic animals, they may now use modern technologies such as guns and skidoos instead of bows and dogsleds, or harpoons and plastic canoes instead of spears and hide kayaks. Similarly, they often live in prefabricated cabins instead of igloos,

Previous pages: An Inuit hunter walks on a summer ice floe beneath the midnight sun. Hunters continue to wear traditional coats made from the hides of reindeer. The fur faces inward to create a cushion of air which is trapped between the leather and the wearer's skin, providing an efficient form of thermal insulation.

Left: The Inuit use a breed of semi-domesticated dog, known as the husky, for hauling their sleds. The dogs are small and compact to suit the severe conditions in the Arctic, and they are used in teams to provide the traction necessary for pulling the sleds, the hunters, and their hunting paraphernalia.

wear synthetic clothing instead of furs and go to school instead of relying on their elders to teach them.

Perhaps inevitably, the Western ethos influences desires and aspirations which can result in a certain dissatisfaction with the old ways of doing things. Some choose to escape their homelands and pursue ambitions in the wider world. Others feel trapped and frustrated by the traditional lifestyle. However, there are many Inuks and Yupiks who find a happy compromise between the old and the new, and maintain a healthy sense of pride about their ethnicity. Indeed, many do relatively conventional jobs to earn their livings, but proudly maintain their ethnic identity by practicing traditional pastimes in their free time, such as hunting, fishing, storytelling, and, of course, conversing in their languages.

In Arctic Europe and Arctic Asia there are other polar peoples. A region known as Lapland comprises the Arctic regions of Scandinavia (Norway, Finland, and Sweden) as well as the Kola Peninsula of Russia, west of the Urals. The indigenous population are known as the Lapps or Laplanders. They speak a language of nine distinct dialects called Lapp, which belongs to the Finno-Ugric linguistic group. The Lapps number around 25,000 and have a culture closely associated with the migratory movements of reindeer herds in the region.

Living east of the Ural Mountains, in north-western Siberia, are the Khanty and Mansi peoples. They speak two languages – Khanty and Vogul – known collectively as Ob-Ugric languages, which belong to the same linguistic group as the Lapp language. They number around 28,000 and 11,000 respectively.

There are also the Samoyed peoples of north-central Siberia. Like the Lapps, they practice a nomadic lifestyle, herding reindeer, hunting, and fishing. They speak several languages known collectively as Samoyedic languages, which belong to the Uralic linguistic group. The largest Samoyed group are the Nenets people, who speak Nenets and number some 27,000. There are also the Selkups, the Enets, and the Nganasans who number around 4000, 250, and 850 respectively.

Penultimately there are the Yukaghir people of north-eastern Siberia. They speak a language of the same name and number approximately 1500. They exist in nomadic tribes, including the Anauls, Chuvans, and Khodyns. Finally, the Svalbard islands, north of Norway, support a population of about 3000 comprising a mix of races, having been in Russian and Norwegian possession.

The total native human population in the Arctic is in the region of 160,000 when indigenous peoples from North America, Europe, and Asia are all taken into account.

Above: The Inuit, as a race of people, display physical adaptations to life in the Arctic environment. They are short and stocky in frame, which provides a low surface area to volume ratio, meaning that their bodies are efficient at conserving warmth.

Right: Physical anthropologists believe that the characteristic narrow eyes of people from oriental stock are another adaptation to life in cold conditions. It has the double advantage of preventing the eyeballs from freezing and reducing the level of reflected sunlight that can enter into the eyes.

Above: This scene demonstrates the way in which the Inuit have managed to combine the old with the new. These people are fishing in a traditional way by dropping a line through a hole in the ice, yet they wear modern clothing and their chosen form of transport is a snowmobile or skidoo.

Top: Four Inuit are seen whale hunting in a traditional boat called an umiak. The boat has a frame made from whale bone and wood, which is then covered with skins of the bearded seal. The white ball is a float to prevent a harpooned whale from making its escape by diving far below the surface of the water.

Above: A traditional way of conserving fish meat is to smoke it. The fumes and heat from smoldering wood chips serve to sterilize the meat and reduce its moisture content so that micro-organisms cannot colonize the surface. Smoked fish will last for long periods when kept dry and cool.

Above: This is a small fishing community in Norway. Villages such as this need to be self-sufficient in the winter months as they are often cut off from the outside world for several months during the winter. Ice, snow, and storms prevent people from either leaving or visiting during this period.

Above: Reykjavik, in Iceland, is the most northerly capital city in the world. The air here is clean – Reykjavik is also the least-polluted capital city in the world. The houses tend to be of wooden construction with lightweight roofs to cope with heavy snowfall.

Following pages: Reindeer are traditionally used to supply commodities such as hides, meat, and milk. But a more recent development has been the introduction of reindeer racing. The reindeer can pull skiers along behind them at speeds of up to 37mph (60km/h).

Below: Volcanic activity affords Iceland a great advantage when it comes to generating electricity. This plant is a geothermal power station, where naturally heated water from below ground produces steam that is used to drive turbines. They, in turn, rotate dynamos to produce electricity.

Above: Hot springs are so plentiful in Iceland that they are capped with valves ready to be exploited whenever they are needed. The majority of Icelandic homes are heated with geothermal water at little running cost to the inhabitants. In some places even the streets are heated to keep them clear of ice.

Left: This is an oil-processing plant in North Slope, Alaska. Crude oil, which derives from the organic remains of ancient oceanic organisms, comprises many different chemicals known as fractions. Heating the crude oil to different temperatures causes the fractions to boil-off separately for collection.

Right: Beneath the Arctic wilderness there are enormous reserves of fossil fuels. This is part of the Trans-Alaska oil pipeline, which is used to carry crude oil from remote oil rigs to refineries where it can be processed into useful fractions including gasoline, kerosene, and diesel oil.

ARCTIC EXPLORERS

It is now believed that the very first humans to set foot on North American soil may have visited from southern France. The Solutreans were Stone Age people who lived on the European continent during the end of the last ice age – the Pleistocene – around 20 thousand years ago. They had a very distinctive stone tool culture and their artifacts have been identified at archeological sites on both sides of the north Atlantic. Anthropologists suggest that they were similar to the Inuit, living at the edge of northern ice fields which extended southward to the middle of France at that period in prehistory. By using boats they were able to travel in short stages across the Atlantic, camping on the ice floes and hunting for food as they ventured eastward.

The next voyagers to cross the Atlantic, and to reach the true North American Arctic, were the Vikings, sometimes known as Norsemen or Danes. They originated from Scandinavian Europe so already knew how to cope with extreme cold. They found their way across in the Middle Ages via Iceland and Greenland, where they set up colonies. Unlike the Solutreans, the Vikings were a true seafaring people, able to sail across open tracts of water using the Sun and stars to navigate their passage.

The modern age of Arctic exploration began in the mid-16th century. Such names as Frobisher, Barents, Hudson, Baffin, Bering, Ross, Franklin and McClintock all took their turns venturing into uncharted territory over a 350-year period. Their principal aim was to discover a viable trade route from Europe to China, so Arctic exploration was largely incidental to their mission. The first person to knowingly stand above the magnetic North Pole was British explorer James Ross in 1831. He found it just north of King William island in northern Canada.

With the turn of the 20th century exploration became more of a matter for national pride and prowess than economic gain. The Norwegian Roald Amundsen became the first explorer to navigate the Northwest Passage (the route between the Atlantic and the Pacific) between 1903-06. He also relocated the magnetic pole for the first time in 1904 only to discover that it had moved by 50 miles (80km) from its previously recorded position. The US explorer Robert Peary became the first man to reach the axial or geographical North Pole in 1909.

Of course it would be unfair not to acknowledge the Inuks, Yupiks, Lapps, and Siberians as the true explorers of the Arctic. Indeed they may very well have achieved all of the above

Above: Robert Peary (1856–1920) became the first person to reach the geographical North Pole on 6 April 1909. In this photograph he is seen wearing polar gear made from furs. On his feet he has wicker snow shoes, designed to spread his weight so that he will not sink into the snow as he walks along.

Opposite: The Arctic explorer Robert Bartlett (1875–1946), is seen here with a group of Inuit in 1909. He was involved with a number of Arctic expeditions alongside Robert Peary and captained the steamer SS *Roosevelt* which carried Peary's 1908-09 expedition into Arctic waters.

milestones themselves, albeit unwittingly, hundreds or even thousands of years earlier. It is, after all, something of a conceit for Western explorers to think of themselves as the original intrepid adventurers when they frequently came into contact with other humans en route for whom the Arctic was their ancestral home.

Above: Roald Amundsen (1872–1928) was beaten in his attempt to be the first man to the geographic North Pole by the success of Robert Peary. He then switched his attentions southward and became the first person to reach the geographical South Pole on 14 December 1911. Here he is seen in 1920 with a sled and team of huskies on a later expedition to the North Pole.

Above: This is not simply a sculptured pile of rocks. It is a traditional Inuit work of art known as an inukshuk, which means 'likeness of a person.' Several inukshuk are 'inuksuit.' They serve different purposes. Some act as markers and pointers to help Inuit hunters find their way about over a predominantly featureless Arctic landscape. Others warn of impending danger or mark a place of respect.

Right: Since Robert Peary's pioneering voyage of exploration in 1909, the geographical North Pole has become relatively easy to reach. This picture shows a party of polar tourists dancing around the northernmost point on the planet as though it were a May pole. A complete revolution of the pole carries a person through all 24 of the world's time zones.

Below: This vehicle is called a tundra buggy. It is a coach mounted on enormous wheels that spread the weight to enable it to travel over boggy ground, where other vehicles would sink in and get stuck. Tundra buggies are useful for transporting Arctic tourists.

Above: For the more adventurous tourist there is the snowmobile or skidoo, which is the equivalent of riding a quad-bike. The very first 'snow tractors' were developed by Robert Scott (1868–1912), who used them initially during his ill-fated expedition to reach the South Pole.

Left: These Arctic tourists are discovering the sensation of walking on the thick clear ice that surrounds October Revolution Island in the Arctic Ocean north of Russia. This region is so cold that it has a mean annual temperature of minus 20°F (-29°C).

Top: The sheer scale of glaciers is illustrated clearly in this image, showing tourists exploring the ice. The deep vertical fissures above them are crevasses that have been exposed side-on. These can be hundreds of feet deep and literally become death traps when people fall into them from above.

Above: For tourists seeking something a little different, the Arctic ice hotel is an intriguing destination. Naturally the temperature inside needs to remain below zero degrees centigrade for the ice to remain frozen, but that is still a lot warmer than the temperatures outside.

Above: This picture shows a hiker gazing down on a colossal glacier, high up in a mountain range in Alaska. People seem to be drawn to such spectacles because they provide a welcome opportunity for reflection. Inevitably humans and their concerns seem comparatively insignificant in such an awe-inspiring setting.

LIFE IN THE WATER

The life that inhabits the Arctic Ocean is remarkably diverse in nature. Ranging in size from gigantic whales to microscopic plankton, a profusion of mammals, fish, and invertebrates have found ways not only of surviving in this very cold environment, but also of thriving and multiplying too.

WHALES

All the fully aquatic marine mammals found in the Arctic today belong to the order known scientifically as Cetacea, the name being taken from the Latin for whale 'cetus.' Whales are broadly divided into two suborders – the toothed whales and the baleen whales. There are nine families, six toothed and three baleen.

Toothed whales are, as one might expect, predatory species, feeding on all manner of marine animals, such as squid, fish, birds, and other mammals. They range in size from dolphins and porpoises, through larger pilot and killer whales up to the massive sperm whales. All species possess teeth in their upper and lower jaws for seizing their prey.

Baleen whales are not predatory for they specialize in eating zooplankton (tiny marine organisms), krill, and small fish, which they filter from the seawater rather than hunt. To do so they use huge plates of whalebone equipped with fibres, known collectively as baleen, for sifting the animals out of mouthfuls of seawater as if through a giant sieve.

The baleen, or whalebone, whales also range in size, but they are generally bigger than the toothed whales. They include right whales, gray whales, and the enormous rorqual species that include the blue whale, the largest animal ever to have lived on Earth.

Whales are mammals, and it is believed that they evolved from terrestrial ancestors that first became semi-aquatic and then fully aquatic over time, so that their limbs adapted from legs into fins and flippers. Whales need to breathe air, because they have lungs instead of gills. This means that they need to rise to the surface frequently and regularly to take in oxygen. They are also warm-blooded and carry their young in a womb, nourished via a placenta.

Each species has its own clearly-defined characteristics which enable it to exploit a certain niche in a challenging environment.

Right: The humpback whale is popular among whale watchers because it readily comes to the surface and has a predilection for spyhopping, fin-slapping, and up-ending when it shows off its tail flukes. It is also a large species of whale, which is easy to identify, and is usually seen in herds.

Left: Pilot whales are so called because they were once used as guides to pilot ships through narrow straits. They weren't tethered to ships or trained to do so, but sailors found that they tended to swim along the deeper water channels, so following them was a sensible precaution as it prevented vessels from running aground.

own lives. Being white below means that killer whales find it more difficult to pick narwhals out against the brightness of the sky above.

The most distinctive feature of narwhals is their tusks, which may have given rise to legends about unicorns. They are usually seen only in the males, but females occasionally have them too. Generally only one tusk grows per adult, but rarely two are seen. The tusks are not horns but teeth that have adapted to grow forward and twist to create long, straight lances, the purpose of which is jousting. Males 'sword fight' to establish dominance, just as male deer lock antlers. Like the beluga, the narwhal is not found all around the polar circle; it is absent between the Alaskan and Siberian peninsulas.

Pilot, Bottlenose, and Killer Whales

These whales are medium-sized species, belonging to two families. The long-finned pilot whale *(Globicephalas melas)* and the killer whale *(Orcinus orca)* belong to the same family as dolphins, and are known rather misleadingly as the 'blackfish group.' The northern bottlenose whale *(Hyperoodon ampullatus)* belongs to the family known as beaked whales.

The blackfish are so called because they are predominantly charcoal or pitch in color, although they also show white or gray markings. They are intelligent and social animals that live in extended family groups called pods. For both species lobtailing

(slapping the water with their tails), spyhopping (raising their heads vertically above the water) and breaching (lunging out of the water and falling back with a splash) are all typical behavior.

Pilot whales feed primarily on squid and fish, so they tend to frequent open deep waters. They can be recognized by their keel-shaped dorsal fins, which have drooping or wilting tips. They grow to about three times the length of a man.

Killer whales, otherwise known as grampuses, are somewhat larger whales. They are more versatile hunters, capable of taking a range of prey, including other whales, seals, sea birds, fish, and squid. In short, they have very wide-ranging tastes. Killer whales often hunt in packs, encircling their prey and tiring it into submission. They can be recognized by their tall, erect, shark-like dorsal fins and piebald markings.

Beaked whales are so called because they possess jaws modified to function in much the same way as the beaks of birds. In the case of the bottlenose whales they have lost all traces of teeth, except for a pair (sometimes four) that protrude from the very tip of the lower mandible. They are known to specialize in eating squid.

The Arctic species has a northern Atlantic range, extending into the Arctic Ocean as far as the Svalbard islands, 400 miles (640km) north of Scandinavia. None of the beaked whales is well known to science, as they inhabit deep waters away from land and are rarely observed.

Above: Killer whales are inquisitive and curious about events above and below the waterline. They are also highly socialized and intelligent like most cetaceans. When they leap clear of the water it is known as 'porpoising' (above), while lifting their heads vertically out of the water is known as 'spyhopping' (left).

Left: Killer whales, or orcas, are intelligent and efficient hunters. They also have comprehensive tastes when it comes to their prey, taking all manner of marine mammals and birds that they encounter during their travels. They can be considered the marine equivalent of wolves hunting for quarry in packs.

Following pages: A killer whale cruises purposefully in the waters off the coast of Alaska. Killer whales are easy to identify because they have a distinctive large, black dorsal fin, which is erect and triangular with a slight backward sweep.

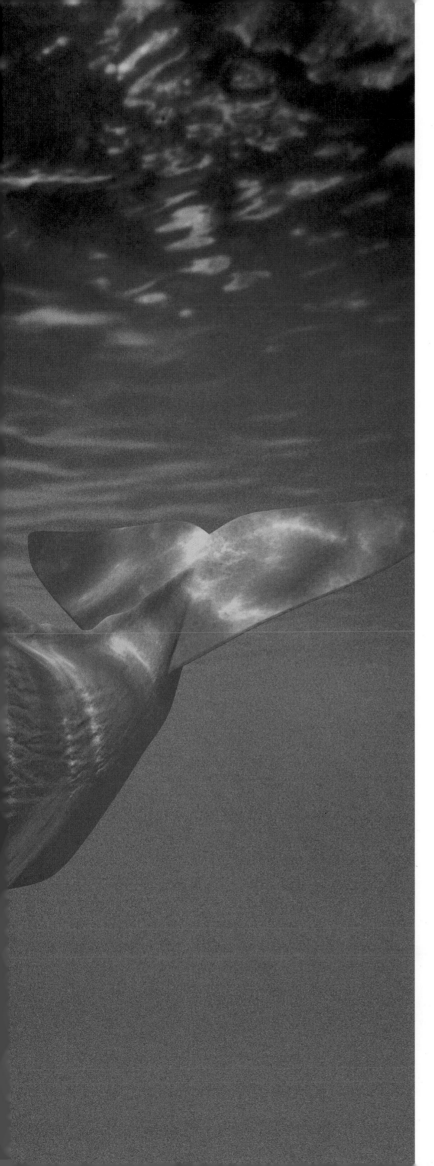

Sperm Whales

The sperm whale *(Physeter macrocephalus)* is something of a legend, because of its reputation as an animal that will put up a dangerous fight to the very end when harpooned by whalers. It was a white sperm whale, named Moby-Dick, that tormented and finally killed Captain Ahab in the novel *Moby-Dick* by Herman Melville. Sperm whale teeth were extensively carved and embellished by whalers in the 19th century and sold as craft souvenirs known as scrimshaw.

The sperm whale is a large – 60ft (18m) long – and robust whale that feeds on giant squid that are hunted at great depths. Specimens often bear the scars of their battles with these squid, which are themselves as much as 60ft (18m) long, so no wonder whalers found them a challenge. Amazingly scientists have only recently managed to photograph a living giant squid for the first time. Yet there must be thousands, if not millions, in the world's oceans as there are still plenty of sperm whales feeding on them, despite the efforts of whalers to exterminate them.

Sperm whales were hunted mercilessly to harvest a valuable white wax, known as spermaceti. Before the by-products of crude and other oils became commercially available, spermaceti was in great demand for the production of candles, ointments, and cosmetics. It is abundant in the head cavities and in the blubber (body fat) of sperm whales, where it is a component of sperm oil – itself once used as a fuel for lamps.

Spermaceti is also found in the whale oil of other species, but not in such large amounts. Another product of their blubber was stearin, and this was processed to make tallow, which in turn was used in the manufacture of soap and glycerol.

Male sperm whales will venture as far north as the Arctic polar ice in the summer months, but females and calves tend to remain farther south. They are seldom seen near to shore, simply because they require deep water to find their food. Schools of sperm whales may contain anything from a few individuals to many hundreds.

Left: Sperm whales are deep sea specialists. Their bodies are superbly adapted to cope with the incredible water pressures encountered when they dive in pursuit of the large squid that make up their staple diet. Their air-filled lungs become compressed to a fraction of their usual size but remain unharmed.

BALEEN WHALES

The baleen whales all feed by filtering or sifting their food from the seawater. This may be zooplankton (sea-dwelling micro-organisms and larvae), krill, or small fish and squid. The whales have enormous gapes with pleated throats, so that they can trap large volumes of water when they close their mouths. They then squeeze the water out through baleen plates, which – rather like a sieve – prevent the food items from escaping. Finally, the tongue is used to scrape off the mass of food into an enormous bolus ready for swallowing.

As a consequence of this method of feeding, baleen whales all share a rather similar design, with pelican-like snouts. They are large whales, ranging from 33ft (10m) to 88ft (27m) in length. Filter feeding must have a high energy and nutrition intake to expenditure ratio to allow these creatures to grow to such enormous sizes. Their huge size also enables them to travel from one feeding ground to another very quickly and efficiently. It also means that the ratio of surface area to volume is low which helps greatly in conserving warmth while swimming in cold waters. In addition to this, huge size is a very efficient form of protection from predators.

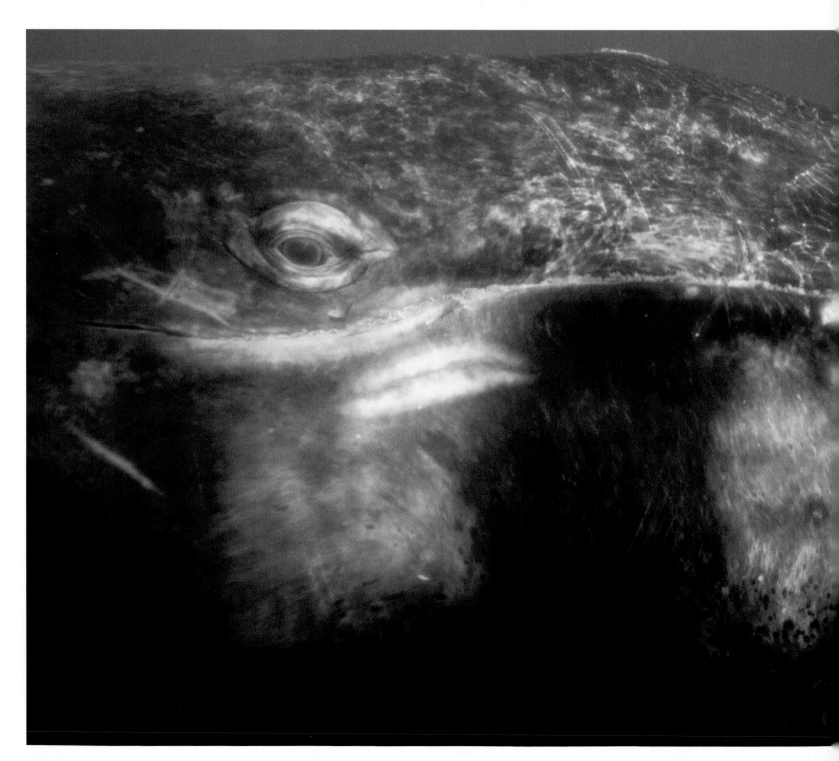

Bowhead, Right, and Gray Whales

The bowhead whale *(Baleana mysticetus)* is a true Arctic species. Its range does not extend all the way around the polar circle though – it is interrupted by the coast of north-eastern Siberia and the islands of Canada. The name alludes to its massive lower lips, which form a bow-like shape.

In the same family is the northern right whale *(Eubalaena glacialis)*. This species only ventures into subarctic waters in and around the Bering strait. It has lower lips which have an upturned 'U' shape and has skin growths on its head which are known as callosities.

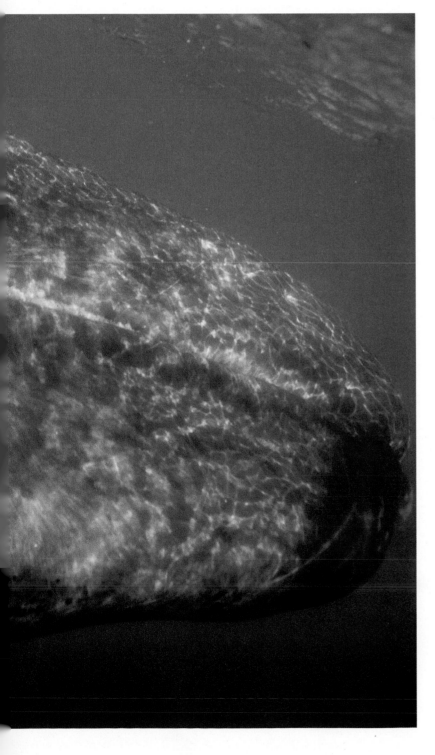

A third species which is similar in appearance, but from the rorqual family, is the humpback whale *(Megaptera novaeangliae)*, so called because its small dorsal fin is situated atop a distinctive hump on the lower back. The genus name *'Megaptera'* translates as 'great winged' because this species has disproportionately large, wing-like front flippers. It enters Arctic waters from both the Atlantic and Pacific oceans.

While the previous three species are predominantly blue-black in overall color, the gray or grey whale *(Eschrichtius robustus)* is, as one might expect, a dull gray-green color. In fact, it generally looks something of a mess, because it typically has a lot of callosities, barnacle growths, and scars on its body. Its unkempt appearance has given rise to other, more pejorative, names, such as devilfish and scrag whale. Another name is mussel-digger, which alludes to its feeding habit of dredging its mouth along the ocean floor to filter out fish, crustaceans, sea urchins, and other invertebrates from the muddy sediment.

The gray whale is a migratory species. Those that reach Arctic waters in summertime, via the Bering strait, travel south to overwinter off the coast of California. Their scars bear witness to their fights with killer whales intent on killing their calves.

In the same family as the humpback whale are the true rorqual whales – genus *Balaenoptera*. Of the five species, four can be found in Arctic waters: the minke whale *(Balaenoptera acutorostrata)*, the sei whale *(B. borealis)*, the blue whale *(B. musculus)* and the fin whale *(B. physalus)*. These whales are far more streamlined than the humpback and other baleen whales, and thus are better able to pursue fast-moving shoals of fish and squid. They have small dorsal fins, set at the back end of the body, and looking rather like the skeg of an upturned surfboard.

Like the sperm whale, the rorqual species suffered heavy losses as a result of whaling in the past, as their sheer size made it profitable for whaling ships to hunt them down. Controlled numbers are still culled by the Norwegian and Japanese factory ships, although primarily as sources of traditional food rather than for their physical by-products.

Left: While the sperm whale might be described as a handsome creature, it has to be said that the gray whale is a far less prepossessing beast. It specializes in harvesting marine organisms that live on the ocean floor. It bulldozes them up by using its lower jaw as a plowshare.

Previous pages: Gray whales are remarkably placid animals. These two specimens are playing with one another, seemingly oblivious to the boat on the left of the picture and the boat on which the photographer is situated. Of course, large whales have few natural enemies to worry about instinctively.

Above: The humpback whale's skin is embellished with wart-like growths, known as callosities. They are caused by colonies of small creatures known as cyamids or 'whale lice,' which infest the skin. Strictly speaking, cyamids are actually crustaceans and not lice, which are flightless insects.

Left: Humpback whales have beaks rather like those of pelicans. This is an example of convergent evolution, as they feed in a similar way. The elastic throat is used to gulp quantities of water containing fish or krill. The water then drains away to leave a mouthful of food.

SEALS, SEA LIONS, AND WALRUSES

This group of animals (scientifically classified in the order Pinnipedia) contains amphibious marine mammals. That is to say, unlike whales, they can still come to land to rest and breed. Their limbs are something of a midway point between flippers and legs, so that they can either use them to shuffle about on land or for steering and maneuvering their bodies gracefully through water.

They are all descended from a carnivorous ancestor and they feed on all manner of marine animals, including sea birds, fish, squid, crustaceans, sea urchins and starfishes, mollusks, other invertebrates, and carrion.

Having made a compromise between aquatic and terrestrial lifestyles, pinnipeds are unable to grow to the enormous sizes that whales do. This is because their skeletons would not be able to support the weight of their bodies when out of water. This is demonstrated clearly by the larger male specimens, which are scarcely able to haul themselves out of the sea onto beaches, rock ledges, and ice floes. Any bigger and they would fail.

Seals

The most ubiquitous genus of seals in the Arctic region is *Phoca*, to which four species belong. They might be described as typical seals, as the family name for all seals is Phocidae. The species present are the harp seal *(Phoca groenlandica)*, the ringed seal *(P. hispida)*, the spotted seal *(P. largha)*, and the common or harbor seal *(P. vitulina)*. They are all fairly small, fish-eating species, ranging from about 4ft (1.5m) to 6ft (2m) or so in length.

Together their range extends right around the polar region. They were once considered subspecies of one species – *Phoca vitulina* – but they are now thought not to interbreed in places where ranges overlap. They can be differentiated only with difficulty, but they do have slightly different pelt markings.

These seals are hunted by indigenous populations for their skins, meat, and other products. Supporters of the hunt argue that the practice is regulated and licensed by the Canadian government, and that seals exist in good numbers. In fact, they are culled in some places to check their numbers because they compete for fish with the local fishing industries. However, conservationist groups, such as the International Fund for Animal Welfare and Greenpeace, oppose the hunt as an unacceptably cruel practice and one that may have unforeseen effects on the population levels of these animals. Apart from man, their wild enemies are polar bears and killer whales.

There are three other phocid, or true seal, species in the Arctic region. The bearded seal *(Erignathus barbatus)*, grows to around 8ft (2.5m). It possesses a bushy mustache of whiskers, rather than a beard, which it uses as a sensory device while feeding on mollusks and invertebrates at the ocean's bottom. It has a gray-to-brown coat and a rather portly frame. The gray seal *(Halichoerus grypus)* is of a similar size and has a dog-like face, minus the ears. It is a fish feeder and bears a blotchy pattern of grays on its coat. The male hooded seal *(Cystophora cristata)* has an inflatable bladder above its nose, which it uses for display purposes. It seems to resemble a large ball when inflated. The males of the species are on average 8.2ft (2.5m) in length, but can

Left: This ringed seal has adopted the classic 'banana' resting pose of typical seals. It has done so to minimize physical contact with the ice floe on which it is perched. This is to reduce loss of body warmth to the ice. Remaining in the water is even more wasteful of body heat.

grow to an impressive 11.5ft (3.5m). Its range wraps around the bottom and sides of Greenland.

Sea Lions

Sea lions are distinguished from seals by their ability to 'walk' on land, as opposed to dragging themselves along. In truth they use their front and rear flippers to form a tripod, so they have to move with a lolloping gait, but they are generally more agile and upright.

The allusion to lions has come about because the males sport hairy manes around their forequarters when they reach sexual maturity. In fact they serve the same purpose that they do in lions – to protect their necks during dominance fights over territories and females.

Steller's sea lion *(Eumetopias jubatus)* is named after Georg Wilhelm Steller, a German zoologist and explorer who described the species during a voyage captained by Vitus Bering, after whom the sea was named, in the late 1740s. Its range extends into Arctic waters via the Bering strait, for it is a species of the north Pacific only. Male specimens grow to a maximum of 11.5ft (3.5m), while the females are somewhat smaller, as is typical in pinnipeds. Their pups are fed on a very rich milk, so that they fatten up quickly as a defense against the chill waters. Even so, there are heavy losses due to predation, drowning, and crushing by careless adults. Sea lions live in colonies on rocky shores, known as rookeries.

Below: These Steller's sea lions are relaxing on some seaweed-covered outcrops of rock known as offliers. The rocks absorb solar radiation due to their dark color, and the sea lions happily use them as radiators to warm their bodies while they rest.

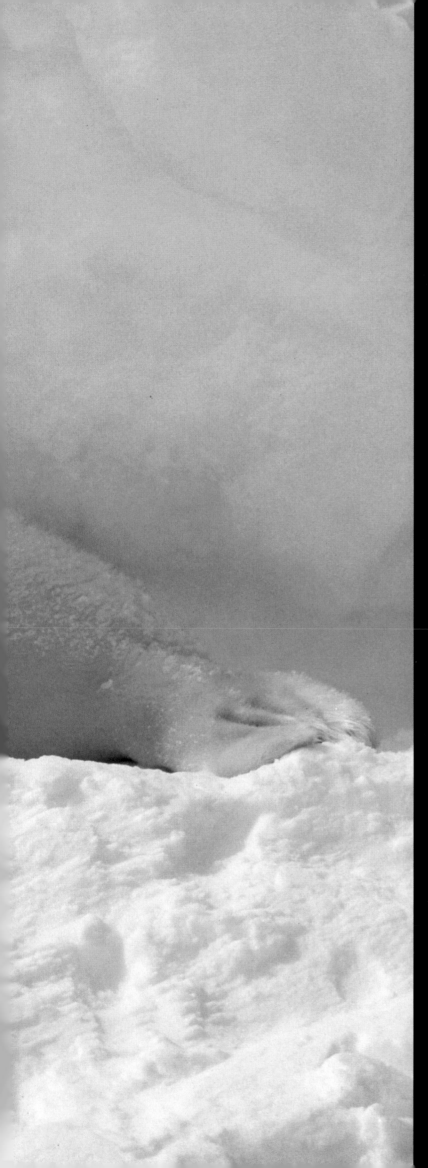

Above: The term 'pinniped' is derived from the Latin for 'wing-foot' (pinna-ped) because seals, sea lions, and walruses have limbs adapted for swimming, like the fins of fish. The flippers of these harbor seals can be clearly seen. Out of water though, they have become virtually useless as a means of propulsion.

Left: This is a harp seal pup, awaiting the return of its mother from a day's fishing. The white fleecy fur acts as camouflage as well as insulation, so that the pup isn't easily spotted by predators. It is fair to say that the pup is utterly helpless at this stage in its development.

Following pages: The colorings and markings on harbor seals are always slightly different from one specimen to the next. It seems likely that individuals are identified by this means, especially when they are out to sea where distinctive scents and sounds are not an appropriate way to tell seals apart.

Walruses

Like the bearded seal, the walrus *(Odobenus rosmarus)* specializes in feeding on mollusks, bottom-dwelling fish, and other invertebrates found on the seabed. Consequently it has the same mustache of bristles which are used for sensing the muddy bottom in the murky depths, where it is too dark to see.

Walruses are virtually hairless over their bodies, but have developed a thick layer of blubber as insulation from the cold. They also have thick, leathery skin as protection from the cuts and grazes that result when they laboriously haul themselves out of the water onto land for the purposes of resting and breeding. Males may reach 12ft (3.6m) while females are around 8ft (2.5m).

Their skin changes color depending on the amount of blood in the small blood vessels near the surface of the skin. While in the water, blood flow near the skin is reduced to conserve warmth, so that the animals appear grayish. While sunbathing, blood floods to the surface to absorb the Sun's warmth, giving the animal a rose-red blush. The species name *rosmarus* alludes to this phenomenon.

Male walruses sport greatly enlarged upper canine teeth – tusks – that can grow to 3ft (1m) long in mature individuals. They are used as sparring weapons during dominance disputes over females and territories. Walruses are found all around the polar circle.

FISH

The Arctic fish world is essentially divided into marine species and freshwater species, although there are those that move between both types of water and others that prefer the brackish (slightly briny) water in estuaries. What they all have in common is the ability to cope with the cold water temperatures that occur more or less all year round.

Despite being cold-blooded like amphibians, fish don't need to warm themselves up to become or remain active and they are all able to stand near-freezing temperatures.

The freshwater fish have to be able to survive water temperatures that drop to 32°F (0°C) in winter. Although ice forms at the surface, the water remains liquid beneath, so the fish stay deep. If the water is flowing, its kinetic energy tends to prevent it from freezing over so readily.

When it comes to seawater, the temperatures can fall much lower. The salt in the water acts as an antifreeze, allowing water temperatures to descend below 32°F (0°C) without freezing. Consequently the bodies of fish need to contain antifreeze agents too. Polar fish have been found to contain combinations of chemical components known as antifreeze proteins (AFPs) and antifreeze glycoproteins (AFGPs) in their body fluids. They allow the fish to survive in subzero conditions by preventing water molecules from forming ice crystals.

Fish are broadly grouped taxonomically into two classes: bony fish and cartilaginous fish. There are many Arctic species from each class. Bony fish species include the Arctic grayling (*Thymallus arcticus*), the Arctic char (*Salvelinus alpinus*), the common whitefish (*Coregonus lavaretus*), the Arctic cisco (*C. autumnalis*), and the Arctic or polar cod (*Boreogadus saida*). Cartilaginous fish species include the Arctic sleeper shark (*Somniosus microcephalus*) and the Arctic skate (*Raja hyperborea*).

The Arctic cod has been recorded at latitudes of almost 85°, which is farther north than any other fish species – just 5° short of the geographical North Pole. Like other species specifically adapted to the cold, it cannot survive water temperatures above about 59°F (15°C). Conversely, there are other fish that visit Arctic waters only in summer months, as they cannot function in temperatures below about 41°F (5°C).

TURTLES

There are also sea or marine turtles that venture into Arctic waters. They have the advantage over land-dwelling reptiles that the ocean waters remain relatively warm. That is to say, the temperatures remain above freezing for most of the year. Green turtles (*Chelonia mydas*) and leatherbacks (*Dermochelys coriacea*) only venture north in the height of summer, when warm currents flow from the south, but loggerheads (*Caretta caretta*) are unique in being partially warm-blooded. They also possess fat layers for insulation, just like whales, so can cope with cold conditions.

Above: Arctic char play an important role in the food chain, by providing food for marine mammals. Most of their eggs are eaten by many other sea creatures.

Right: Unlike fish, which are also cold-blooded, sea turtles are not able to function when temperatures fall below a certain level, so they only venture into Arctic waters during the summer months.

Opposite: Walruses are the pinniped equivalent of the gray whale. They too specialize in feeding on bottom-living organisms. They use their tusks to hoe the ocean floor in search of crustaceans.

LIFE ON LAND

Many terrestrial mammals inhabit the Arctic region because the Arctic Circle crosses a large area of landmass comprising the northern parts of North America, Europe, and Asia. With plenty of land situated above and below the Arctic Circle, mammals are free to migrate northward and southward with the seasons. So many species find themselves on the list by virtue of their proximity to the Arctic region. They are perhaps better described as subarctic species to distinguish them from those mammals that venture deep into the Arctic for some or all of the polar year.

Around 100 species of mammal are found in the Arctic. They are all placental mammals as marsupial mammals only exist in Australasia and South America. Placental mammals are so called because they gestate their offspring via a placenta in the womb. The young are then born into the world in a well-developed condition and further nourished by milk produced from mammary glands.

Other types of terrestrial animal are also able to lead their lives successfully in the cold conditions of the Arctic, and these include various reptiles and amphibians. There are invertebrates too. The majority are insects but other groups are represented, such as arachnids (spiders and mites), crustaceans (woodlice), diplopods (millipedes), chilopods (centipedes), mollusks (snails and slugs), and annelids (earthworms).

ARCTIC CARNIVORES

There are a number of families from the carnivore order present in the Arctic and subarctic. They are the wolves and foxes, the cats, the weasels, and the bears. Undoubtedly the bears are the most physically awe-inspiring of all the carnivores, and one of them – the polar bear – is forever linked in the public mind with the icy wastes of the Arctic.

Polar Bears

There are three bears in the Arctic region – the black bear *(Ursus americanus)*, the brown or grizzly bear *(U. arctos)*, and the polar or ice bear *(U. maritimus)*. Black and brown bears occupy territory well within the Arctic Circle, but the polar bear is uniquely adapted to a life almost entirely spent on the ice sheets floating above the Arctic Ocean.

The polar bear is so well suited to the polar landscape that its fur is white, which undoubtedly serves as a useful camouflage whilst hunting for whales and seals from above or below the waterline. The white color is something of a happy accident though, as the hair filaments are actually transparent. This helps them to trap solar energy which helps to keep the animals warm in the cruel Arctic conditions of the extreme north.

Previous page and right: At first glance it would seem that the Arctic landscape has little to offer the polar bear by way of food. Certainly potential sources of food are few and far between, but the polar bear is able to kill and consume large prey and so sate its appetite for considerable periods until new hunting opportunities arise.

In the popular consciousness the polar bear is synonymous with the Arctic because it so clearly belongs to the terrain of ice and snow. In addition, its image is frequently romanticized in children's story books about life at the North Pole. Of course, being a strictly polar animal, there is no getting away from this association, but the polar bear is anything but a friendly and cuddly animal.

In fact, it is a ruthless killing machine, capable of hunting down animals bigger than itself and gorging on their flesh. It needs to be, for without the killing streak it would be unable to survive in such an extreme environment. These bears can easily wander for weeks without encountering food, so they have to make certain of a kill when the opportunity arises.

Although they are opportunistic feeders, they specialize in preying on marine mammals – members of the seal and whale families. Their technique is one of ambush and surprise. Seals and whales need to breathe air at the surface of the ocean, and this is the weakness exploited by the polar bear. It sits by the edge of pack ice or near a breathing hole and waits patiently until its quarry comes within striking distance.

A sudden lunge into the water enables the bear to seize the head of the prey animal with its ferocious jaws. A wrestling match then ensues until the animal is dead from drowning, shock, or injury. The corpse is then dragged up onto the ice and feasted upon. A recently fed bear is quite literally 'in the pink' as its fur gets covered in blood that stains its head and forequarters.

In order to make the most of the summer months, female polar bears give birth in wintertime. They build dens by burrowing into snow banks and curling up inside, allowing more snow to build up above them, which acts as insulation from the Arctic weather outside. The newborn cubs are kept in the mother's lap and suckled until springtime arrives. The females then break out of their ice cocoons and begin hunting and foraging for food once again, having relied entirely on their fat reserves during their maternal confinement.

Previous pages: This polar bear has just hauled itself from the water onto an ice floe. This requires a great deal of strength in the upper body, not least because the bear's water-laden coat is heavy. The bear's feet are partially webbed which help it to move easily through the water.

Right: One of the principal threats to polar bear survival is now thought to be global warming. Bears typically hunt seals from frozen ice floes, but milder weather is delaying the onset of the freezing conditions that they rely on to hunt their prey. Scientists are already observing declining birth rates and increased mortality.

Above: Although polar bears have no natural enemies, being the top Arctic predators, it doesn't mean that their cubs are entirely immune to danger. Adult males have been known to attack and cannibalize young cubs. Growing bear cubs generally stay close to their mother until they are two years of age.

Opposite: Polar bears might easily be called marine or aquatic bears, for they are very adept at swimming. They have to be, because most of their prey is caught in water. They can travel quite prodigious distances in the water; some have been observed in the sea more than 100 miles (160km) from land.

Left: Polar bears typically have litters of two cubs. After mating, the female survives on her own. Most of the 240-day gestation period is spent hidden in a snow den, where the female shelters and rests over the winter to conserve energy. She then gives birth and initially rears the newborn cubs held on her warm belly.

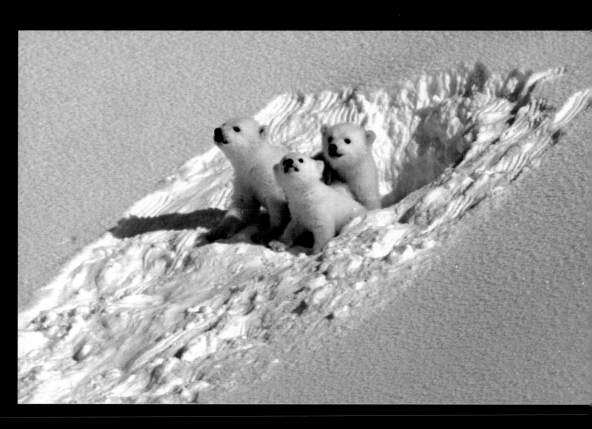

Above: When the cubs are old enough to see and walk unaided, they are allowed to venture from the den for the first time. The young are reared on their mother's milk which is extremely high in fat to help them gain weight rapidly.

Left: Polar bear cubs are very small and helpless at birth, only opening their eyes after about one month. They start eating solid food at 4-5 months of age.

Previous pages: In the wild few easy meals are on offer. Here a number of brown bears are transfixed by the prospect of grabbing leaping salmon in their jaws. Bears are opportunistic feeders with very comprehensive tastes, so fish is just one of many seasonal foods on the menu in the Arctic.

Right: This brown bear's patience has been rewarded with a juicy fish. Salmon travel upstream in huge numbers to spawn. Even though large numbers are taken by bears and other animals, enough complete the journey to ensure that new generations of salmon survive to populate the rivers and oceans.

Above: This is the black bear. It is smaller than the brown bear and employs slightly different foraging techniques. For example, it is better at climbing trees, where it can feed on nestlings and eggs. It is also partial to the honey and grubs of wild bees, whose nests are often found in tree hollows.

Wolves, Foxes, and Cats

Canid species include the gray wolf *(Canis lupus)*, the coyote *(C. latrans)*, the silver fox *(Vulpes vulpes)*, and the Arctic fox *(Alopex lagopus)*. They are all dog-like carnivores, primarily hunters and scavengers of meat, but prepared to supplement their diets with invertebrates and vegetable matter. Foxes hunt alone, while wolves and coyotes organize themselves into packs. A fifth species is the raccoon dog *(Nyctereutes procyonoides)*. It is something of an anomaly – as well as resembling a raccoon, it is the only canid able to climb trees and hibernate.

The Arctic cat species are the Siberian tiger *(Panthera tigris)*, the American lynx *(Lyns canadensis)*, and the Eurasian lynx *(L. lynx)*. They are all solitary by nature and more strictly carnivorous than the canids.

Another diverse group of animals includes weasels, stoats, polecats, martens, mink, sables, badgers, otters, and wolverines. As a general rule, they all have elongated and slender bodies adapted to the pursuit of prey in confined circumstances, whether that be below ground, in water, or up trees.

The genus *Mustela* includes those species described as weasels, stoats, polecats, and mink, of which there are half a dozen representatives distributed around the polar region.

Similarly, the genus *Martes* includes the handful of marten and sable species, and *Lutra* is the genus name for the river otters. The common badger *(Meles meles)* occupies Arctic Europe, while the wolverine *(Gulo gulo)* replaces it in the Arctic regions of Asia and North America.

Above: The coyote is a smaller version of the wolf. Indeed, it is also known as the prairie wolf or brush wolf. Coyotes sometimes hunt as packs members, and sometimes in pairs or even individually, depending on the availability of food.

Left: The wolf is found all around the polar region and is divided into a number of races. Not surprisingly the Arctic version has a white coat to suit hunting in a snow-covered landscape. Its fur is also longer and thicker to provide additional insulation against the cold.

Opposite: The Arctic fox is the smallest of the Arctic canid species. It is adapted to hunting Arctic birds and mammals, such as ptarmigan and lemmings. Its feet are protected from the cold ice and snow by a thick covering of fur.

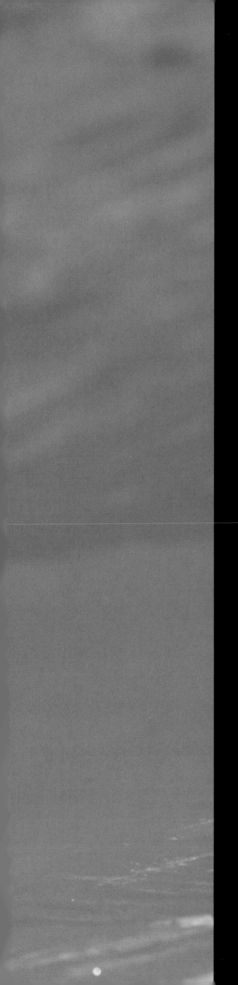

Above: The wolverine is something like a cross between a badger and a marten. It is about 43in (110cm) long and weighs around 55lb (25kg). It is equally at home hunting on the ground or up trees, which has the advantage of providing it with two hunting grounds within a single habitat.

Left: This white wolf, like so many other Arctic animals, has its own snow shoes. The feet are enlarged to spread the weight of the animal more effectively when walking on soft snow. In addition, the paws are extremely furry to provide even more surface area.

Following pages: This Siberian tiger is shown in its ideal habitat. It is easy to see that when hidden in the grasses behind it is very well camouflaged. It is the perfect cover for ambushing deer, which are its favorite prey animals. Regrettably, because of illegal hunting, this magnificent creature is now on the brink of extinction.

ARCTIC HERBIVORES

The even-toed ungulates are split-hoofed animals such as wild sheep, deer, and cattle, although different common or familiar names are often used for species within these groups.

There are two subarctic sheep species – one from the Old World and one from the New World. They are the Siberian snow sheep *(Ovis nivicola)* and the Dall snow sheep *(O. dalli)* respectively. Both are whitish in color and similar in behavior. They live in rocky terrain where they graze and forage for grasses and other foliage.

Sheep belong to the same family as cattle, which are represented by the muskox *(Ovibos moschatus)*. It is a cow-sized animal with low-slung horns and a shaggy coat. Muskoxen inhabit the Arctic tundra wastes of northern Canada and many of the islands east of Greenland, which become linked by ice during the winter months.

The best-known Arctic deer are the elk or moose *(Alces alces)* and the reindeer or caribou *(Rangifer tarandus)*. Both species are found across both North America and Eurasia. Reindeer are about 6ft (2m) long and live in large herds, which have been exploited by nomadic human populations for thousands of years. The herds migrate in pursuit of good seasonal grazing, and where they go, the humans have to follow. Elk are giants among deer, sometimes reaching 11.5ft (3.5m) in length. They roam the landscape alone or in small family groups. Both species sport antlers as adults, but only the males do in the elk's case.

Other subarctic deer include the common and Siberian roe deer *(Capreolus capreolus* and *C. pygargus)* and the Siberian muskdeer *(Moschus moschiferus)*. These species are more typically deer-like in appearance as they are not adapted to tolerate true Arctic conditions.

Below: The moose is a very large species of deer. In the winter months moose feed on just about any edible plant matter they can find. This includes dead grasses, herbs, mosses, lichens, and twigs.

Left: Despite appearances, the muskox is more closely related to goats than to cattle or true oxen. The muskox can be seen as a survivor of the last ice age, as it is known to have grazed alongside woolly mammoths and rhinos.

Below: Theses animals are described as mountain sheep, rather than mountain goats, because they have a fleecy coat and their horns have a space between them at their base. They are Dall or thin-horn mountain sheep. Both males and females possess horns, but the rams' horns are thicker.

Left: This is a large deer called a wapiti. It is sometimes known as the elk, but this name is also used for the moose in certain parts of the world. Unlike the moose, the wapiti is more typically deer-like in appearance. It has a straight muzzle and the tines of its antlers are not webbed.

Above: Most species of deer travel in pairs or in small groups, but reindeer herd together in their hundreds. This is because they are more strictly migratory than other deer, and it helps to travel with the reassurance of safety in numbers. Reindeer herds have been farmed for centuries by the indigenous people of the Arctic region.

Left: Muskoxen are so robust that they have no need to run from predators. When threatened, they form defensive corrals with their calves protected within. This is effective against wolves and other natural foes, but less so against a human threat.

SMALLER ARCTIC MAMMALS

It may come as something of a surprise to learn that bats manage to survive in the subarctic region, but there are a few species on record. They are all insectivorous feeders, so they have to take advantage of the seasonal glut in flying insects over the spring and summer months. Some species are semi-migratory, but they all hibernate to survive the winter months.

The best represented genus is *Eptesicus*. It contains species commonly known as big brown or house bats. An example is the northern bat *(Eptesicus nilssoni)* of Scandinavia. It is resident just 62 miles (100km) from the Arctic Circle.

The name insectivore is rather misleading, as insects make up only a relatively small proportion of the diets of animals in the insectivore order. Other invertebrates, such as worms, mollusks, crustaceans, arachnids, and sometimes eggs, fish, reptiles, and amphibians, make up the greater part of it.

Shrews of the genus *Sorex* are by far the most numerous insectivores found the subarctic and Arctic regions. There are half a dozen species, such as the Arctic shrew *(Sorex arcticus)*. They are famed because they need to eat their own body weight in food each and every day to survive. There are also water shrews of the genus *Neomys* and moles of the genus *Talpa* that make a living in the subarctic.

Hares, like rabbits, are often mistaken for rodents, but they belong to a different order despite appearances. It has to be said, though, that the differences between hares and rabbits and rodents are subtle. For example, hares and rabbits have four instead of two incisors in the upper jaw. The third and fourth are known as peg or secondary teeth and are situated immediately behind the first and second incisors. This enables them to graze on short grasses by gripping the blades between their lower incisors and the slot above, something rodents cannot do.

In the Arctic the predominant genus is *Lepus*, which contains the typical hares. There are a few species, of which the Arctic hare *(Lepus arcticus)* is a good example. Like the polar bear, it is very well adapted to polar conditions, even turning white in winter to help avoid the attention of predators. Its range includes northern Canada, parts of Greenland, and many of the islands inbetween.

There are also pikas which are rather like rabbits, but with small rounded ears. The northern pika *(Ochotona hyperborea)* lives between crevices in rocky terrain. It seems that rabbits are absent from the Arctic only because the ground is unsuitable for digging burrows.

Above: There are no Arctic rabbits because the tundra is too hard to allow them to dig burrows. Arctic hares get by above ground, which is why they have to be so well camouflaged against the backdrop of snow. When predators are detected, the hares literally lie low, so that they cast little or no shadow.

Right: While similar species, such as the mountain hare and snowshoe hare, molt into their white coats for winter, the Arctic hare remains white all year round. It has evolved to stay white because it lives in regions where snow is a permanent part of the landscape.

Below: Pikas are really rabbits that have adapted to life among the boulders and moraines of the Arctic habitat. Their smaller size means that they are better suited to squeezing into crevices and burrowing into pockets of soil where they make their nests.

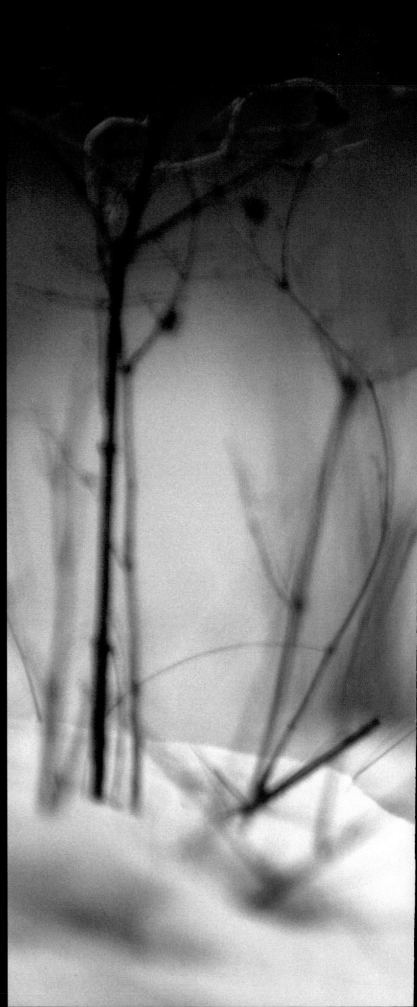

Above: Marmots are variously known as rock chucks and whistle pigs. They are actually ground squirrels that make their homes in extensive burrow networks beneath hillside rocks and boulders.

RODENTS

In the Arctic there are more than 50 species of rodent to be found. They include voles, mice, rats, tree squirrels, lemmings, beavers, muskrats, marmots, chipmunks, ground squirrels, porcupines, woodchucks, and flying squirrels.

They vary in size from 2in (5cm)-long voles to the 3ft (1m)-long beavers. Some species live in trees, while others are terrestrial or semi-aquatic. They have perpetually growing and very sharp incisor teeth that make light work of plant tissue, including leaves, stems, roots, nuts, fruits, and even bark and wood. Gnawing at things keeps their incisors sharp and worn down to the right length. If they gnawed too much, then their teeth would be worn to stumps and they would have to wait for them to grow again. If they gnawed too little, then their teeth would outgrow their mouths and make it impossible for them to feed. All are strictly vegetarian with the exception of rats.

Undoubtedly the most famous rodents of the Arctic are the lemmings, which are like large voles. There are a dozen species described as lemmings and belonging to four genera, although the true lemmings belong to the genus *Lemmus*, the tundra or Norway lemming *(Lemmus lemmus)* being the type species. Examples from the other genera are the northern bog lemming *(Synaptomys borealis)*, the wood lemming *(Myopus schisticolor)*, and the arctic lemming *(Dicrostonyx groenlandicus)*.

Lemming populations increase rapidly when food is plentiful during favorable weather, as they can reproduce with vigor. This fact has led to one of the wonders of the animal kingdom – lemming migrations. When resources become exhausted, large numbers of lemmings have no choice but to travel in search of food. Momentum gathers as numbers swell in an increasingly desperate bid to escape starvation, so that vast swarms of frenzied rodents stop at nothing in their path. The result is that many millions perish by drowning and exhaustion until a natural balance between population density and the availability of food is once again restored.

Another genus of rodents that is frequently found is *Microtus*, which contains the typical voles. There are around ten species,

Above: Beavers are among the few animals that use technology to adapt their environment, just as humans do. They build dams across rivers, so that lakes of floodwater build up. This allows them to get at submerged plant material for food and for building lodges.

Right: Ground squirrels are adapted to life on terra firma, where they live in communal burrows. The Arctic ground squirrel is the only Arctic mammal that truly hibernates. It fattens itself up over the summer and then becomes dormant until springtime.

Left: Chipmunks are ground squirrels that belong in a separate genus from the Arctic ground squirrel. They are distinguished by the striped markings on the sides of their heads and torsos. Chipmunks frequent forested areas south of the tundra zone. Some chipmunks hide seeds in their winter chambers and will interrupt their period of hibernation to feed on the cache of food.

such as the tundra vole *(Microtus oeconomus)*. Like the lemmings, voles are distributed around the polar region. Other voles include the lemming vole *(Eothenomys lemminus)*, the water vole *(Arvicola terrestris)*, and bank voles *(Myodes* species).

The remaining rodents comprise a wide assortment of creatures including marmots or woodchucks *(Marmota* species), gophers or ground squirrels *(Spermophilus* species), beavers *(Castor* species), porcupines *(Erethizon* species), flying squirrels *(Pteromys* species), chipmunks *(Tamias* species), tree squirrels *(Tamiasciurus* and *Sciurus* species), jumping mice *(Zapus* species), wood or field mice *(Apodemus* species), typical rats *(Rattus* species), and the muskrat *(Ondatra zibethicus)*.

REPTILES

Reptiles do not adapt very well to Arctic conditions. This is simply because they are cold-blooded, which means that their temperature varies with that of the environment around them. Consequently, reptiles are largely dependent on the warmth of their habitat to provide the energy they need for survival. Although their food provides energy in its raw state, their metabolism doesn't generate the heat necessary for digestion and the maintenance of constant body conditions as it does in warm-blooded mammals and birds. They therefore require ambient warmth and heat from the Sun to get their internal processes going. Once they are active, then a certain amount of warmth is generated internally by the movement of muscles.

Needless to say, truly Arctic conditions leave precious little opportunity for reptiles to avoid freezing up, let alone move about to find food and breed. Nevertheless a few species do exist as far north as the Arctic Circle or just below it. They make the most of the brief season when it is warm enough to go about their lives and then hibernate underground for the rest of the time. This clearly isn't possible beyond the point at which the permafrost begins.

The subarctic species include the viviparous lizard *(Lacerta vivipara)* and the slow worm *(Angius fragilis)*, and the grass snake *(Natrix natrix)* and the garter snake *(Thamnophis sirtalis)*.

The term 'viviparous' means to bear live young, as opposed to 'oviparous' which means to bear eggs, which most reptiles do. In fact, to confuse matters even more, viviparous lizards are 'ovoviviparous' which means that they bear live young, but from eggs incubated within the body. This strategy has the advantage of allowing the lizards to begin the process of reproduction early on, when it would still be too cold to lay eggs. Garter snakes are ovoviviparous too.

Slow worms lay eggs in nests within burrows and they get around the problem of providing ambient warmth by incubating the eggs with their bodies. Grass snakes incubate their eggs by laying them within piles of rotting vegetation, so that the warmth generated by the decomposition of the plant matter does the trick.

AMPHIBIANS

Although amphibians, like reptiles, are cold-blooded, they can function at lower temperatures, and are therefore more numerous in subarctic conditions. Reptiles are ectothermic, which means that they need to absorb heat from their surroundings before they can find the energy to liven up, unlike mammals and birds which are endothermic – they generate their own body heat. Amphibians, like fish and invertebrates, do not require much thermal energy to become or remain active.

Frogs and toads are represented by several species of frog from the *Rana* genus and several toads from the *Bufo* genus. Examples are the wood frog *(Rana sylvatica)* and the boreal toad *(Bufo boreas)*. The wood frog is so well adapted to Arctic conditions that it hibernates by allowing itself to freeze entirely. In effect it preserves itself in a cryogenic state, as its heart and brain stop working until it thaws out in the springtime. Actually, the frog has glucose in its cells, which act as an antifreeze down to about 19°F (minus 7°C), so that the water does not form ice crystals that would rupture the cells and kill the animal. Another species with glucose antifreeze is the boreal chorus frog *(Pseudacris maculata)*. In fact all subarctic amphibians need similar defenses against freezing.

There are also newts and salamanders present in the Arctic. Unlike the frogs and toads, they have tails in both their larval and adult stages. Species examples are the great crested newt *(Triturus cristatus)*, the rough-skinned newt *(Taricha granulosa)*, the northwestern salamander *(Ambystoma gracile)*, and the long toed salamander *(A. macrodactylum)*.

Frogs and toads tend to hibernate beneath layers of leaf litter and snow, while newts and salamanders are inclined to do so in the muddy substrate beneath iced-over water. Each of these strategies ensures that temperatures don't fall too low, even if conditions in the outside world above are truly severe.

All amphibians require freshwater to breed. Their eggs are laid in the water and hatch into larvae called tadpoles or pollywogs. Those of newts and salamanders can be distinguished from those of frogs and toads by their feathery gills and the early development of four legs, which make them look a little like miniature dragons with ruffs.

Above: Amphibians, such as this wood frog, are cold-blooded, but they don't need to warm up like reptiles do in order to become active. In this respect they are more like fish. Nevertheless, they come equipped with antifreeze in their blood and body cells to prevent freezing up during cold winter conditions.

Left: Reptiles, such as this garter snake, are few and far between in the Arctic, simply because they are cold-blooded and prefer warmer climates. Those that do manage to survive in the far north tend to be very dark in color, so that they optimize the absorption of solar radiation by their skin.

ARCTIC BIRDS

The birds that inhabit the Arctic are diverse in their nature and behavior. Some are seabirds that live along the coastlines and find their food out at sea, others are waterfowl, shorebirds, birds of prey, and even varieties of songbird.

AUKS

Just as the southern hemisphere has its penguin family, so the northern hemisphere has its auks. The penguins and auks are an example of a scientific phenomenon known as convergent evolution. Despite their being only distantly related, they have adapted in similar ways to suit similar econiches. To all intents and purposes they fill the same roles in the Arctic and Antarctic habitats.

The auk family contains 22 living species and one that was driven to extinction in the mid-19th century. They are subdivided into 12 genera and are variously described as auks (*Alle* species), razorbills (*Alca* species), guillemots (*Uria* and *Cepphus* species), murrelets (*Brachyramphus* and *Synthliboramphus* species), auklets (*Ptychoramphus, Cyclorrhynchus, Aethia* and *Cerorhinca species*), and puffins (*Fratercula* and *Lunda* species).

The species that died out was the great auk (*Alca impennis*). It lived in enormous numbers in and around the north Atlantic.

The great auk was an outsized razorbill species that had lost the power of flight, and this was to prove its undoing, because it fell victim to the feather industry. For hundreds of years sailors and explorers had exploited the great auk as a source of food, in the form of meat and eggs, but as the population numbered in the tens of millions, it had never been significantly affected. Then in the mid-1700s there came a demand for feathers to stuff bedding across the Western world. The industry lasted 100 years, until the last great auks were killed in 1844 on an island off Iceland.

The original name for the great auk was the penguin. The name was later adopted for the penguin family because of the uncanny similarity that sailors and explorers noticed in their appearance and behavior. In addition of course, there were no more real penguins left alive. The name 'penguin' was apparently derived from the Latin *'penna-gigno'* meaning 'feather-provider.'

Most auk species frequent Arctic and subarctic coasts and waters, either in the north Atlantic or north Pacific. They can all fly, although they have much reduced wings, so have to flap them very quickly to achieve flight and remain airborne. This is an evolutionary compromise, because they also need to use their wings as flippers for propulsion and steering while submerged in pursuit of the fish, squid, and crustaceans on which they feed, and under water their small size is an advantage.

Previous page: The razorbill is perhaps the archetypal auk species. This is the blueprint design from which all other larger and smaller species have evolved. It is certainly very similar to the fabled great auk. A population of tens of millions of these birds was hunted to extinction in the north Atlantic.

Above: This is the tufted puffin, which frequents the northern Pacific, just as the Atlantic puffin resides in the northern Atlantic and Arctic. There is a third species – the horned puffin – which covers areas on the Siberian and Alaskan coasts. All three species overwinter far out to sea.

Right: Puffins are members of the auk family. The auks typically have black and white plumage, but the puffins alone have evolved multicolored bills. It seems likely that they indicate breeding fitness, as a horny sheath develops in the springtime to display the bright colors and then sloughs in the fall after the breeding season.

Above: The most diminutive of the auks are known as auklets, of which there are a number of similar species. These crested auklets are sporting extravagant plumes of feathers above their bills, which serve as indicators of breeding fitness to impress and attract other auklets of the same species.

Left: Guillemots are very similar to razorbills in overall form, but they are slightly more gracile and have slenderer bills. Razorbills and guillemots often nest in mixed colonies, making it easy for ornithologists to compare and distinguish the two visually.

WATERBIRDS

There are nearly 200 species of waterbird recorded in the Arctic and subarctic regions. They are all migratory to some extent, as they move away from the Arctic in winter to find food elsewhere.

All ducks, geese, and swans are essentially herbivores that graze plants in and out of water. They will also eat insects and other invertebrates as a supplement to their diets. These birds are waterfowl with fully webbed feet and flattened bills, and range in size from small to large. There are around 50 Arctic species.

The duck tribe is broadly divided into diving or sea ducks and upending or dabbling ducks. The first group includes goldeneyes and buffleheads (*Bucephala* species), eiders (*Somateria* species), scoters (*Melanitta* species), canvasbacks, redheads, ring-neck ducks, tufted ducks, and scaups (*Aythya* species), goosanders, mergansers, and smew (*Mergus* species), the harlequin (*Histrionicus histrionicus*), Steller's eider (*Polysticta selleri*), and the long-tailed duck or old squaw *(Clangula hyemalis)*. The second group includes mallards, wigeons, teal, pintails, shovellers, and gadwalls (*Anas* species).

The geese are from three genera: *Anser* (gray geese), *Branta* (brown geese), and *Chen* (snow geese), while the swans belong to the genus *Cygnus*, such as the tundra swan *(Cygnus columbianus)*.

Divers and grebes are superficially similar to ducks and geese, except that they have pointed bills and legs set so far back on their bodies that they have difficulty walking on land. This is an adaptation to diving for food. The black-throated diver or Arctic loon *(Gavia arctica)* is one of half a dozen Arctic species and has a distribution all around the polar region. The most ubiquitous grebe is the golden-horned *(Podiceps auritus)*. Divers and grebes have omnivorous diets including small fish, amphibians, and aquatic invertebrates.

Another family of duck-like birds comprises coots and rails, which are similar to grebes, except that they have their legs set beneath their bodies, making them able to walk and balance very well on water plants. They are birds of marshland and bog, with

Opposite: Many waterfowl migrate to and from the Arctic tundra on a seasonal basis. During the summer months tundra swans take advantage of the brief glut of new plant growth and aquatic insects, which they gather to feed their cygnets. Adults and young then migrate south for the winter.

lobed feet for spreading their weight. The coots, such as the common coot *(Fulica atra)* and the American coot *(F. americana)* are rather bold in behavior, while the rails, such as the water rail *(Rallus aquaticus)*, are rather more shy and secretive.

Cormorants are goose-like birds of marine habitats with hooked bills for seizing fish. They have a habit of drying their wings after diving by holding them away from their bodies, because their feathers lack the oils that other waterbirds use to waterproof their plumage. The shag cormorant *(Phalacrocorax aristotelis)* is found in the waters of Iceland and Lapland where it may spend many hours of every day diving for food.

The northern gannet *(Morus bassanus)* is the one member of its family found in Arctic waters. It resembles a very large gull and makes spectacular dives from high in the air into the ocean in search of fish. Its range extends into Icelandic and Scandinavian waters.

Gulls and tern belong to the family Laridae. Gulls of the genus *Larus* are numerous in the Arctic region. There are a dozen species that cover just about every habitat that the region has to offer. They are typically white birds with grayish backs and black

Above: The snow goose population comprises three distinct subspecies: the white snow goose (pictured above), the blue snow goose, and the lesser snow goose. Evidently populations of the species became genetically isolated in the past, so that they evolved to look slightly different in size and color.

wingtips. Examples are the herring gull *(Larus argentatus)*, the glaucous gull *(L. hyperboreus)*, and the Iceland gull *(L. glaucoides)*. Other Arctic gulls include Sabine's gull *(Xema sabini)*, the ivory gull *(Pagophila alba)*, the kittiwake *(Rissa tridactyla)*, and Ross's gull *(Rhodostethia rosea)*.

Terns are similar to gulls in their coloration but are smaller and slighter in build. They plunge-dive for small fish, such as sand eels. The Arctic tern *(Sterna paradisaea)* is remarkable for having the longest migration of any animal. It breeds within the Arctic Circle, yet it overwinters in the Antarctic region. This remarkable round trip amounts to around 21,750 miles (35,000km) every year.

Above: Kittiwakes are members of the gull family, but they are adapted to life on precipitous cliff faces, where they nest alongside auks, such as razorbills and guillemots. Their name is imitative of their call, which is quite unlike the typical squawks and mews of most other gulls.

Skuas or jaegers are very similar to gulls in form and habit, except that they are mainly brown instead of white. They specialize in harrying other seabirds into dropping their food. There are several species in two genera. The Arctic skua *(Stercorarius parasiticus)* and the great skua *(Catharacta skua)* are typical examples.

There are a number of birds including the northern fulmar or petrel *(Fulmaris glacialis)* and the Manx shearwater *(Puffinus puffinus)* collectively known as tube-noses, because they have tube-like nostrils mounted above their bills. The birds possess glands for extracting the salts from seawater and the saline waste product is ejected through the tubes. They are skilled fliers, able to stay on the wing for long periods of time.

Above: The Arctic tern is famed for its migrations between both polar regions. It seems likely that such migrations began at a time when the last ice age brought the polar environments far closer together. Subsequently the terns had farther to travel each year as the ice caps retreated.

Above: Cranes, such as this sandhill crane, are generalist feeders among the shorebirds. They have long, bare legs to suit wading in fairly deep water, where they can feed on all manner of aquatic animals that live above and below the waterline. They will take fish, amphibians, reptiles, small mammals, insects and other invertebrates.

Left: The Arctic loon is also known as the great northern diver. Here a parent bird is seen with a juvenile. Loons are so well adapted to their aquatic habitat that they are reluctant to come ashore for fear of ambush by predators. They prefer to nest on small islands for safety's sake.

Left: Despite appearances to the contrary, the fulmar is not closely related to the gulls. It is actually a miniature albatross. This is evident

Left: The wigeon can be distinguished from other related ducks by its pure white speculum, which is a patch of color on the secondary flight feathers of the wing, which is visible while at rest as well as in flight. It is thought that the name 'wigeon' is a contraction of 'water pigeon' as the duck is rather pigeon-like in plumage.

Below: This is a raft of king eider. The drakes are the showy looking specimens, while the ducks are those with cryptic coloring. This is typical among ducks as the females use their camouflage to avoid being spotted by predators while they incubate their eggs. The males patrol the area away from the nest.

SHOREBIRDS

The North American term 'shorebird' is synonymous with the term 'wader' used in Europe. Shorebirds are all birds with proportionately long legs for wading in shallow water and typically with long bills for probing in mud, silt, and sand to find food. Shorebirds or waders belong to two large orders of birds – one comprises the smaller types, such as sandpipers and plovers, and the other contains the larger types, such as cranes and herons.

Around 50 Arctic shorebirds belong to the sandpiper family. As well as sandpipers, it comprises species known as godwits, curlews, redshanks, greenshanks, phalaropes, turnstones, snipe, stints, knots, yellowlegs, dunlin, dowitchers, ruffs, sanderlings, whimbrels, tattlers, and surfbirds. They typically have long legs for wading in coastal shallows, where they search for worms, crustaceans, and mollusks. Their bills come in an array of shapes and sizes which is an indication that they each specialize in hunting food animals from slightly different econiches on beaches and mudflats.

Birds from the genera *Calidris* and *Tringa* account for more than half of the sandpiper species in this region. Examples are the purple sandpiper *(Calidris maritima)* and the green sandpiper *(Tringa ochropus)*. There are more than a dozen other genera.

The phalaropes *(Phalaropus* genus) are of biological interest, as they exhibit gender role reversal. The males exhibit quite dull coloration and tend the eggs and young, while the females are brightly colored and display.

The Eskimo curlew *(Numenius borealis)* is worth a mention too, as it may have been hunted to extinction. There used to be countless millions of the birds in North America until unrestricted hunting for food in the late 19th century saw their numbers reduced to a critical level. By the 1970s they were thought to have been lost altogether, but new sightings were made in the early 1980s. Since then no confirmed sightings have been made. The birds migrated between the Arctic tundra and the US grasslands, which have since been used for growing crops. So sadly the additional habitat loss seems to have sounded the Eskimo curlew's death knell.

Similar to sandpipers, but with shorter bills, are the members of the plover family. Species are variously known as plovers and killdeer *(Pluvialis* and *Charadrius* species), lapwings *(Vanellus* species) and dotterels *(Eudromias* species). There are about ten Arctic species. They also have shorter legs and relatively larger heads than sandpipers.

Another small family of shorebirds contains oystercatchers, with robust reddish bills, designed for probing at mollusks, crustaceans and worms hidden in rock pools and crevices. Examples in the far north are the Arctic and Siberian races of the common oystercatcher *(Haematopus ostralegus)*.

Cranes are bigger wading birds that feed on larger prey, such as fish, frogs and insects. The species here belong to the genus of the typical cranes – *Grus*. They include the common crane *(Grus grus)*, the sandhill crane *(G. canadensis)* and the Siberian crane *(G. leucogeranus)*.

Above: The curlew uses its curved bill to probe deep into mud and sand for food. Shorebirds' bills vary in shape because they each specialize in feeding on different prey to avoid direct competition for food. The curlew is able to reach deeper into mud and sand than most other species of shorebird.

Following pages: Small shorebirds, like these sandpipers, typically travel and feed in large flocks. Such flocks can also comprise several species. This is an example of strength in numbers, as it is a very effective way of confusing predators that might otherwise be able to hunt down an individual bird on its own.

BIRDS THAT LIVE ON LAND

Not surprisingly, there are just as many terrestrial birds in the Arctic and subarctic as there are waterbirds – somewhere around 200 species at least. Terrestrial birds are divided into two broad camps: passerine birds, otherwise known as perching birds, and non-passerine birds.

Just to make matters more confusing, passerines are further divided into oscine passerines and sub-oscine passerines. The former are primarily 'Old World' birds (meaning that they are originally from Africa-Eurasia) and have fully developed voice organs for singing. They are otherwise known as songbirds. The latter are mostly 'New World' birds (species from the Americas) though not all, and they have less well-developed voice organs. They are sometimes known as calling birds. The passerines are a very numerous order, accounting for 60 percent of all bird species.

All passerines, or perching birds, share a mechanism in their legs which locks their toes under the weight of their bodies. This enables them to perch with no muscular effort. Conversely, the toes loosen their grip as soon as the weight is lifted and the ligaments are slackened. This explains how the term 'perching bird' was coined.

The smallest passerine species are the goldcrests (*Regulus* species) while the largest species are the ravens (*Corvus* species). Most species are, therefore, small to medium-sized birds.

Passerines

Passerines are small perching birds that tend to go unnoticed by those who are not particularly interested in birds. A good many have dull plumage too, especially the females, which doesn't do an awful lot for their popular image! They are affectionately known by ornithologists as SBBs (small brown birds).

Warblers are good examples of this dull uniformity as it is often difficult to tell species apart even with a trained eye. There are two families of warblers. One contains the Old World warblers, such as the Arctic warbler (*Phylloscopus borealis*), where the other contains the New World warblers, such as the yellow-rumped warbler (*Dendroica coronata*). Both families are filled with countless species, all generally brown and olive in color.

A similar group are the wagtails and pipits. Unlike the warblers, which are tree-dwellers, these birds are ground-living and nesting. They habitually twitch their long tails as they run about looking for food. Examples are the citrine wagtail (*Motacilla citreola*) and the rock pipit (*Anthus petrosus*). They are associated with the shoreline, where they prey on flying insects and other small invertebrates.

There are also two families of flycatchers – one from the Old World and one from the New. Flycatchers, as their name suggests, specialize in catching flying insects. They typically fly sorties from favorite perches where they sit in an upright posture so that they have the best view of the area. The spotted flycatcher (*Muscicapa striata*) and alder flycatcher (*Empidonax alnorum*) are examples from each family.

When it comes to seedeaters things get a little confusing. Two families comprise the Old World sparrows and finches, while a third family contains the New World equivalents, which are usually called either sparrows or buntings. Examples from the three families are the tree sparrow (*Passer montanus*), the chaffinch (*Fringilla coelebs*), and the rustic bunting (*Emberiza rustica*).

The medium-sized passerines of the Arctic region belong to the thrush family. As well as the thrushes, this family includes a range of smaller birds, such as the bluethroats and rubythroats

Above: This is a boreal chickadee, otherwise known as a titmouse or tit. Chickadees eat insects and eke out a living during the winter months by searching trees for dormant invertebrates. They are so small that they are able to get by on the tiniest morsels.

(*Luscinia* species), redstarts (*Phoenicurus* species), the solitaires (*Myadestes* species), and wheatears (*Oenanthe* species). They all have the typical 'thrush' shape nevertheless. The genus *Turdus* contains the typical thrushes, such as the redwing *(Turdus iliacus)* and the fieldfare *(T. pilaris)*. Species from other thrush genera include the hermit thrush *(Catharus guttatus)* and the varied thrush *(Ixoreus naevius)*.

The large Arctic passerines belong in the crow family. It is loosely divided into crows, magpies, and jays. The crows are generally gray-black, while the other family members are piebald or two-tone in appearance. They all have somewhat rasping calls rather than songs. Arctic species include the hooded crow *(Corvus cornix)*, the common magpie *(Pica pica)*, and the Siberian jay *(Perisoreus infaustus)*.

In contrast with the crows, the smallest passerines are the tits, yellow-crests, and wrens. They are all tiny birds that specialize in feeding on small invertebrates, such aphids, caterpillars, and spiders, that are hidden in foliage.

Above: This yellow-rumped warbler is among many small passerines or perching birds that venture into the Arctic to take advantage of the huge numbers of flying insects that emerge each spring. Evidently the migration from farther south is a worthwhile exercise for these small birds.

Left: Crows are opportunists and scavengers. This individual is on a reconnaissance flight to see whether the polar bear might leave a few scraps of food for it to pilfer. This type of feeding behavior requires a certain amount of cunning and intelligence, which crows possess in no small measure.

Non-passerines

The terrestrial birds that aren't passerines form a far more varied group, for they belong to many different orders rather than just the one. Perhaps the best adapted to the Arctic environment are the grouse. Grouse are so well suited to the snow and ice that they don't migrate like most birds. Instead they molt and develop white plumage as a camouflage to protect them from predators. Good examples of this are the rock ptarmigan *(Lagopus mutus)* and the willow grouse *(L. lagopus)*. Even in summer they have speckled plumage as camouflage to make them blend into the rocky background.

Among the most deadly enemies of grouse, and of other birds and small mammals, are the birds of prey. There are two orders in this group: the owls and the falcons, hawks, and eagles. Loosely speaking, the former are nocturnal birds and the latter hunt by day, but in the Arctic those rules don't apply strictly because of the prolongation of daylight hours in the summer.

The owl species vary in size and diet to avoid direct competition with one another. They typically prey on small to medium-sized mammals and birds, although they will also take worms and other invertebrates. Most northern owls are large species, as this makes them better able to cope with the cold

conditions, especially if they are resident in winter. The genus *Bubo* contains the eagle owl (*Bubo bubo*) and the great horned owl (*B. virginianus*), while the genus *Strix* contains the great gray owl (*Strix nebulosa*) and the Ural owl (*S. uralensis*).

The hawk owl (*Surnia ulula*) is very hawk-like indeed and specializes in chasing down passerine birds. The classic Arctic owl is the snowy owl (*Nyctea scandiaca*), which has white plumage as camouflage against the snow. It makes a living from hunting small mammals, especially lemmings.

Snowy owls are ground-nesting birds, as they inhabit areas of tundra where suitable trees are absent from the landscape. They have enemies in the form of larger mammal predators, but these owls are large and powerful birds, able to defend their eggs and chicks very effectively.

To save energy while hunting, snowy owls will take up position on vantage points, such as mounds and hills, where they will sit and survey their surroundings. As soon as they detect movement in the undergrowth, they take to the air and swoop down for the kill. As well as lemmings, they will also take Arctic hares and grouse, and other small mammals or birds.

The other birds of prey are conveniently divided into subgroups, based on size and wing shape as well as other taxonomic details. So we have eagles (*Aquila* and *Haliaeetus* species), buzzards (*Buteo* species), hawks (*Accipiter* species), harriers (*Circus* species), falcons (*Falco* species), and the osprey (*Pandion haliaetus*).

The different species of raptor vary in size which means that they can specialize in hunting certain types of prey and avoid direct competition with one another. All kinds of quarry are taken, including mammals, other birds, reptiles, amphibians, fish, and invertebrates.

In the forested areas of the subarctic band there are quite a few woodpecker species, as the habitat is perfect for them. Woodpeckers are well adapted to a life feeding on the wood-boring larvae of beetles and moths. They have powerful bills for drilling into wood and clawed feet for holding themselves fast on the tree trunks.

Members in the type genus *Picoides*, include the three-toed woodpecker (*Picoides tridactylus*) and the downy woodpecker (*P. pubescens*). Species from other genera include the black woodpecker (*Dryocopus martius*), the northern flicker (*Colaptes auratus*), and the spotted woodpeckers (*Dendrocopus* species).

Birds that have similar lifestyles are the treecreepers (*Certhia* species) and nuthatches (*Sitta* species), although these are both in passerine (perching) families. As a rule of thumb, treecreepers work trees in the upright position moving from bottom to top, while nuthatches work them in the upside-down position, from top to bottom. In this way, they are able to exploit different food resources located in the same habitat. Similarly woodpeckers exploit the food resource beneath the bark of trees.

Remarkably, there is even a species of kingfisher in the Arctic. The belted kingfisher (*Megaceryle alcyon*) has a range that extends well into the Arctic region of North America during the summer breeding season. It is a large species, at 14in (35cm) long, and is able to tolerate cooler temperatures. It takes advantage of the seasonal glut in small fish in the streams that lead north to Arctic waters.

Opposite: One of the top predatory birds is the magnificent golden eagle. This large bird is able to kill prey as big as deer, so it has a considerable range of quarry available to it. Conditions during the winter months can work in the eagle's favor by making it more difficult for victims to escape.

Above: This is a rock ptarmigan, or grouse, in its cryptic summer plumage, which ensures that it is camouflaged against the background of rocks and stones on the mountain side. In winter the rock ptarmigan's plumage becomes pure white, except for a black tail and black band between each eye and the bill.

Right: The willow ptarmigan, or grouse, is darker brown than the rock ptarmigan in its summer plumage, but virtually indistinguishable in its winter whites. Except, that is, for the detail that it lacks any black on its face, as can be clearly seen here. Both ptarmigans are sometimes known as snow hens.

Above: The belted kingfisher may seem an unlikely Arctic visitor, but the summer brings an abundance of small fish that the bird can exploit to feed its young. In this species the female is more colorful than the male, as she has reddish flanks and chest band. Such gender reversal is comparatively rare in the bird world.

Left: The gyrfalcon is a formidable bird of prey, being the largest of the falcon species. The northern race has this white base color, but southern races are gray-brown. It hunts by flying over the ground at great speed, so that ground birds and mammals are caught unawares by the element of surprise.

Following pages: The snowy owl is adapted to life in the Arctic tundra, where there are no trees in which to nest. This means that it has no choice but to nest on the ground. This is a female, as the males have far fewer black markings. She is sitting on her nest to provide warmth for her concealed eggs or chicks.

THE ANTARCTIC

*A*s the Apollo 17 spacecraft headed for the Moon in December 1972, a crew member looked back toward Earth and took the famous full-disc photograph of our blue planet with its brightly lit southern icecap gleaming through space. This is Antarctica – the coldest and loneliest place on Earth. The Antarctic continent itself is entirely covered by a layer of ice over 1.2 miles (2km) thick. Amazingly, this constitutes 70 percent of the freshwater in the world and 90 percent of the world's ice. This is a land of extremes where conditions can be ferociously harsh.

The average temperature in the interior is around

minus 49°F (-45°C) and wind speeds of up to 200mph (320km/h)

have been recorded around the coast. It is no surprise, therefore, that

very few animals can overwinter on the ice, and the lack of an escape

route to warmer climes explains why the wildlife found in the

Antarctic is less diverse than that found in the Arctic. But, as we

shall see, the animals and plants that do manage to survive 'life in

the freezer' are every bit as fascinating and remarkable as their

northern counterparts…

THE ANTARCTIC LANDSCAPE

The motion of the Earth around the Sun has exactly the same influence on the Antarctic as it does on the Arctic. To appreciate this fully, try not to think of the Earth as having a right way up. In astronomical terms, there is no real top or bottom. We could just as easily think of the Antarctic as being at the top of the planet. The same angles apply whichever way around we mentally place the two poles. They both experience the same deprivation of sunlight in winter and the same overexposure to sunlight in the summertime, but the seasons are always six months apart.

What really makes the Antarctic and Arctic different from one another is that they are diametrically opposed in terms of their geography. The Antarctic is a landmass surrounded by ocean, while the Arctic is an ocean surrounded by landmass. Antarctica is a continent in its own right, surrounded by the Southern Ocean, whereas there is no Arctic continent, but only the Arctic Ocean surrounded by the continents of North America, Eurasia, and Greenland. This geographical difference makes them very disparate places indeed.

From a botanical and zoological point of view, Antarctica is a more remote prospect in terms of terrestrial life forms. The Antarctic Circle virtually frames Antarctica's coast, so that the only significant piece of land that straddles the Antarctic and subantarctic zones is the peninsula that juts out toward the southerly tip of South America. Even there, the terrestrial animals and plants cannot migrate or disseminate very far north before meeting ocean, so they have to be truly adapted to the polar environment.

Only birds and marine animals are able to move to and from Antarctica with the changing seasons, and so these animals do not have to evolve specifically in order to survive the extreme conditions at harsher times of the year.

From a climatic viewpoint Antarctica behaves differently from its northern counterpart too. Every summer a great deal of the Arctic ice sheet melts away, because warmer water currents allow heat energy to melt the ice from below, and so more and more ocean is exposed. On Antarctica things are different, because water currents only affect the ice shelf around the landmass. The inland ice sheet remains intact and continues to reflect away the solar energy, so that most of Antarctica is perpetually frigid.

Right: Antarctica's frozen formations take on an infinite variety of shapes and sizes, because the ice and snow are eroded by different environmental factors such as high winds and warm air currents.

Antarctica is a continental landmass with a surface area of some 5.5 million square miles (14 million km²). That is slightly bigger than Australia. It consists almost entirely of bare rock covered in ice. The ice extends beyond the landmass which increases the surface area considerably, although this extent varies depending on the season. Only about 1 percent of the land ever becomes free of ice, at the tip of the Antarctic peninsula.

Antarctica covers about 5–7 percent of the world's surface, yet it contains 70 percent of its freshwater. Not all of it is ice though, as there are many freshwater lakes beneath the ice, which remain liquid at 32°F (0°C). The ice sheet itself is truly colossal in volume – 5.9 million cubic miles (24 million cubic kilometers) and represents about 90 percent of the world's total ice. It has an average thickness of 1.3 miles (2.1km) and reaches 3 miles (5km) in places.

The interior of Antarctica is a very hostile environment. Temperatures can fall to minus 94°F (-70°C). When wind chill factor is included too, then things get very cold indeed. At the peninsula, however, surface temperatures do rise above freezing point, so that a thaw occurs in summer which allows for terrestrial plants and animals to eke out a living there. The prevailing cold means that Antarctica is 'drier' than the Sahara desert. It has less liquid water available to organisms, because it is virtually all ice and snow. In some interior regions there are 'dry valleys' where ice and snow are absent. The bare rock surfaces seem sterile, but they harbor communities of extremely resilient cyanobacteria and algae.

Antarctica has a number of significant geographic features. Mount Erebus, on Ross Island, is the world's most southerly active volcano. It rises to 12,450ft (3794m) and has been active since 1972. It has a permanent lava lake in its crater. When it was discovered by James Clark Ross in 1841, the volcano was erupting, so Ross thought the name appropriate as Erebus is a Greek god who personified darkness and chaos.

Much of the ice on Antarctica is more-or-less stationary, so that new snow fall has added layers of ice over time. The bottom layers may be as ancient as a million years old. In other places,

Right: This is a bird's eye view of the crater atop Mount Erebus, the most southerly active volcano on the planet. It is a forbidding place, where the air is filled with smoke and steam. As well as these, invisible gases rising from the lava lake permeate the atmosphere.

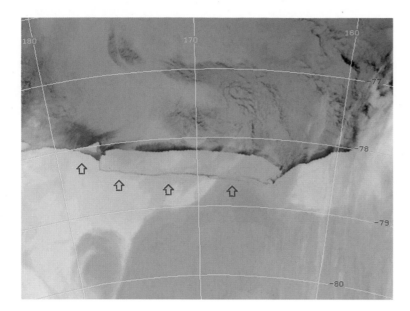

Above: This extraordinary picture is a satellite image looking directly down on Antarctica. The elongated rectangle at the center is a truly enormous iceberg that has just separated from an ice shelf. It is an unbelievable 183 miles (295km) long and 22 miles (35km) wide.

Right: Here is a cliff face made entirely from ice. It is the truncated end of a glacier that feeds ice inexorably into the ocean like a colossal conveyor belt. Layers of dark colored contamination can be seen. These are probably layers of volcanic ash that fell out of the air onto the ice many thousands of years ago.

the ice flows northward toward the Southern Ocean in the form of enormous glaciers. They become truncated to form immense ice cliffs where they meet the ocean. The glaciers are perpetually – albeit very slowly – on the move, so that vast sections of cliff fall away where it meets the sea to form icebergs as an ongoing process. This phenomenon is known as 'calving,' because the icebergs drop down suddenly and rapidly into the sea like newborn calves. They also make extraordinary noises as the ice stresses and strains, giving them an eerie 'living' quality.

The Ross Ice Shelf is where several glaciers meet and join forces to create an 500-mile (800km) wide plateau of moving ice some 188 thousand square miles (487 thousand km^2) in area. That's a floating delta of ice almost the size of Spain or France.

In terms of its geology, Antarctica has an interesting history. It used to part of the megacontinent Pangaea hundreds of millions of years ago and then was part of the southern supercontinent Gondwanaland, which broke up about 180 million years ago to form South America, Africa, India, and Australasia as well as Antarctica. Remarkably, Antarctica was originally nowhere near the South Pole, but lay in equatorial latitudes. It was once densely forested with trees. Fossils and coal deposits testify to this. The continent spent millions of years slowly drifting southward before arriving at its current position. By about 45 million years ago it was cooling down. Australia and New Zealand broke off but

Antarctica continued its march southward. Nearly all of the terrestrial species then died out and the continent was scraped clean of its soils by the action of glaciers.

Antarctica comprises six tectonic plates joined together. East Antarctica (Greater Antarctica) is formed of one ancient plate, while West Antarctica (Lesser Antarctica) consists of five younger plates. The rock types constituting Antarctica are a mix of sedimentary, metamorphic, and igneous. Potentially valuable minerals present there include coal, oil, palladium, and platinum, although extracting them in an economically viable way would be impracticable given the environmental conditions. In any case, an international agreement has existed since 1991 which prohibits the exploitation of Antarctica's mineral resources for 50 years: i.e. until 2041.

Right: Emperor penguins are remarkable creatures – they are the only animals (excluding research scientists!) that can survive winter on the Antarctic continent. They are the largest of the penguins and for good reason. They need bulk to provide a body core able to maintain a sufficiently high temperature to survive the Antarctic winter. Any smaller and they would freeze to death.

ANTARCTIC ISLANDS

Scattered around the continent of Antarctica, or Greater Antarctica as it is sometimes called, there are a great many islands. Some lie within the Antarctic Circle, while others lie on or just outside it. These are known as either subantarctic or periantarctic islands. A few islands are isolated, but most lie in groups or archipelagos. They are frequently accompanied by numerous islets, rocks, and stacks, which are too small to qualify as islands in their own right and are known collectively as 'offliers' because they 'lie off' the coast.

Geologically speaking, the islands fall into two types. There are those of seismic origin and those of sedimentary origin. In other words, some are the peaks of submarine volcanoes, while others are the peaks of submerged fragments of continental crust. Depending on their latitude, the islands often have areas of permanent ice cover or glacierization. Many support terrestrial and marine life of one kind or another.

The most extensive archipelago lies off the coast of the Antarctica peninsula. It is called the South Shetland Islands and comprises a chain of four island groups stretching 325 miles (540km). There are 11 major islands and a plethora of smaller ones.

The largest individual island is Desolation Island or Grande Terre, which is one of the Isles of Kerguelen which are situated in the southern Indian Ocean. It has a surface area of 2577 square miles (6675km²) – about the size of the State of Delaware. Other archipelagos include the South Orkney Islands, the South Sandwich Islands, and the Balleny Islands.

Just as there is the Antarctic Circle, there is also a second boundary line named the Antarctic Convergence or the Antarctic Polar Frontal Zone. This line is not circular as it delineates the position of an irregular boundary between currents of water, but it does form a complete loop around Antarctica. It is where the colder Antarctic waters sink beneath the warmer waters from the north. The boundary is actually about 25 miles (40km) wide and is always in flux, but it doesn't deviate more than 50miles (80km) or so from its mean position. The intermixing of cold and warmer waters in this zone creates local variations in weather and also results in a higher concentration of marine plant life.

Needless to say, the position of islands in relation to the Antarctic Convergence has an influence on their microclimates. The temperature of the water can vary on either side of the boundary by 9–18°F (5–10°C) and this has a marked effect on both the marine and terrestrial habitats of the islands.

Above: The landscape of the South Orkney Islands is still very barren and icy even though portions of the islands thaw out during the summer months. Plants and animals have only a short window of opportunity to get on with the business of growth and reproduction.

Following pages: This icescape is so bizarre that it might appear in a surrealist painting. The elegantly shaped formations in the foreground are icebergs. They are able to stand because they have large bases of ice hidden below the surface of the water.

PLANT LIFE

Plants in Antarctica have to cope with some very particular problems in order simply to survive. As well as the obvious problem with sub-zero temperatures, there is the shortage of water. Although there is plenty of ice and snow, it doesn't become physically available to plants until it has melted into liquid water. In addition to this, the air tends to be very dry, so that evaporation of moisture from plants is a hazard.

Added to these problems is the sparseness of suitable soil in which to put down roots. For the most part there are escarpments of bare rock, with the occasional fissure and crevice filled with organic detritus – a blend of humus and guano – rich in nutrients but thin on the ground.

Consequently there are only two flowering plant species on Antarctica proper. They are the Antarctic hair grass (*Deschampsia*

Above: These rocks are embellished with the burnt orange color of *Xanthoria* lichens, which festoon their surfaces. They grow best on the vertical faces of rocks where they are not trodden underfoot by birds and are able to optimize the levels of sunlight they receive from a low Antarctic sun.

antarctica) and the cushion pearlwort (*Colobanthus quitensis*), both of which grow on the peninsula. They have successfully colonized the region by growing in clumps wherever the soil is deep enough to permit their roots to gain a foothold.

A more successful group of plants are the bryophytes: mosses and liverworts. They are non-flowering plants that produce spores instead of seeds. The advantage of spores is that they can be produced in their millions and they are microscopically small, so that they find their way into any potential place where they might begin to grow and find purchase. The disadvantage is that, unlike seeds, spores don't come with their own food supply to help with germination.

There are approximately 100 species of moss and 30 species of liverwort found on Antarctica. Both classes of plant lack true roots. Instead they secure themselves to the ground with root-like threads, called rhizoids. This enables them to colonize places that would be out of bounds to flowering plants. Species include the silver moss (*Bryum argenteum*) and the Antarctic leafy liverwort (*Cephaloziella exiliflora*).

Antarctic mosses contain chemicals called xanthophyll pigments which are useful to the plants because they help to reflect away the harmful ultraviolet rays in sunlight. They are the pigments that become evident in deciduous plants when the chlorophyll which gives the leaves their green color breaks down in fall, leaving the leaves yellow-brown. In the case of Antarctic mosses, they overproduce the pigments when growing in highly exposed sites, so that the leaflets turn shades of reds or browns, instead of their usual greens.

A few species of fungi have been found on Antarctica, but they are unable to photosynthesize their own food, lacking the chlorophyll of flowering plants and mosses and liverworts. This means that they have limited scope as free-living plants, so far more species live in partnership as lichens. Lichens are symbiotic organisms formed by the association of a fungus and an alga or a blue-green bacterium (cyanobacterium). The fungus is able to extract essential trace chemicals from the surface of the rock. The alga or cyanobacterium is able to photosynthesize food. By swapping resources, they manage to eke out a modest living and grow, albeit very slowly indeed. In some cases lichens manage about 0.04in (1mm) a decade. Around 250 species of lichen are listed from Antarctica, where they colonize the surfaces of rocks.

The mosses and lichens make a colorful addition to the ecosystem in Antarctica. They include the burnt-orange lichen (*Xanthoria elegans*), the black-pitch lichen (*Buellia frigida*), the

purple-red moss *(Ceratodon purpureus)*, the bright-green moss *(Bryum pseudotriquetrum)*, the brown lichen *(Lecanora dancoensis)*, the yellow lichen *(L. intricata)*, and the olive-green moss *(Grimmia antarctica)*.

Many Antarctic lichens contain a protein which enables them to photosynthesize in the very high ultraviolet radiation levels experienced in Antarctica. They use it instead of chlorophyll, which is why they aren't green.

The *Xanthoria* lichen species are interesting – they are part fungus, part alga, and part cyanobacterium. The cyanobacteria produce a red pigment, which captures the light energy safely and then passes it on to be photosynthesized. The lichens also contain an orange pigment, which reflects harmful ultraviolet light away. The combination of red and orange pigments gives the *Xanthoria* lichens their distinctive burnt-orange hue. Other lichens contain the orange pigment too, and they appear in various shades of yellow, orange, and brown. *Xanthoria* lichens also have a coating of a waxy substance called perslaven. It serves to protect

Above: Antarctic fur seals are seen lying amidst clumps of tussock grass which grows freely along the coastal fringes of the subantarctic islands. This robust plant can grow up to 6.5ft (2m) in height.

the organisms from ice during the winter by acting as an antifreeze layer. It also absorbs warmth during the summer to assist in growth. Antifreeze agents are present in all Antarctic lichens.

Algae themselves, although not really plants, are nonetheless very successful organisms in the Antarctic. Colonial or multicellular species include seaweeds and sea lettuces, which grow on the shoreline of the peninsula. There is a terrestrial moss-like species – *Prasiola crispa* – which grows in large green mats. In fact, around 700 terrestrial and aquatic species are listed.

An interesting effect of algal growth is the coloring of snow. Algal blooms are more familiar in water, but they can also marble the snow in shades of green, red, orange, and gray. Most snow

algae are single-celled, but a few are multicelled. Others are filamentous algae or not algae at all, but actually cyanobacteria which may be turquoise, rusty, or black in color. Snow algae include *Chloromonas/Chamydomonas, Chlorosarcina, Desmotetra* and *Ulothrix* species. The colors are produced by concentrations of the organisms themselves and their dormant spores (zygospores). For example, *Desmotetra aureospora* has golden zygospores, while *D. antarctica* has yellow-green ones and *Chloromonas rosae* has red.

There are also colorful ice algae that manage to grow on the underside of pack ice. They are more properly known as diatoms and haptophytes. They also make up the marine phytoplankton (tiny plants that live in the oceans) and therefore form the foundation of the food chain, for they are grazed by Antarctic krill *(Euphausia superba)* and ice krill *(E. crystallorophias)* and their larvae. Krill are diminutive shrimp-like crustaceans, but they live in such huge numbers that they are believed to be the most successful species on the planet in terms of their weight or biomass. Something like half a billion tons of krill are estimated to live in the Southern Ocean. This is enough to feed the countless millions of fish, birds, and marine mammals which prey on the krill.

Opposite: A variety of tundra plants growing on the island of South Georgia. Tundra flora has to cope with growing in a shallow layer of defrosted soil, which is largely humus with little mineral content. Despite the permafrost below there is little free water for the plants.

Above: Krill are crustaceans similar to shrimps and prawns. Krill are vitally important to the food chain in Antarctic waters as they support directly and indirectly (via the fish link) many higher predators, including penguins, seals, and whales.

A CONTINENT FOR SCIENCE

Scientists appreciate that Antarctica is an environment that is extremely sensitive to the effects of changes in the biosphere of the globe as a whole – whether they be related to pollution levels or temperature levels. For this reason there are many Automatic Weather Stations (AWS) dotted around the continent that supply data to the Antarctic Meteorological Research Center, at the University of Wisconsin-Madison.

Some 2500 international scientists, researchers, and support personnel live temporarily on Antarctica. They inhabit three main ice stations. One is situated at the geographical South Pole and is called the Amundsen-Scott South Pole Station. The others – the McMurdo and Palmer stations – are positioned on the coast. McMurdo Station sits on the southern tip of Ross Island and Palmer Station sits on Anvers Island just north of the Antarctic Circle.

In addition to their meteorological work, the field workers also research the biology, geology, and hydrology of the continent. So some scientists are concerned with the flora and fauna of Antarctica, while others are studying its mineral composition and others monitor the movements of pack ice and glaciers.

In addition, important work goes on related to pollution levels, the ozone hole, meteorites, ice core sampling, and marine fertility. In essence, all of these areas of study and connected in one way or another, so that each scientist adds something important to the overall picture of what is happening to Antarctica and what this means for the rest of the planet.

THE OZONE HOLE

Ozone is a naturally occurring trace gas which is unstable, highly oxidizing, and toxic. It has a pungent odor and is pale blue in color. It is an allotropic form of oxygen. Instead of the more usual oxygen molecules that comprise two atoms – O_2 – ozone comprises three atoms – O_3. It is formed from normal oxygen in the atmosphere by the action of ultraviolet light or by the electrical discharge of lightning.

The ozone layer, or ozonosphere, is a natural concentration of the gas at an altitude which varies between 6-30 miles (10-50km) above the Earth's surface in a zone known as the stratosphere. It absorbs potentially harmful ultraviolet radiation from the Sun and so acts as a shield, keeping plants and animals safe from the damage that overexposure to UV radiation can cause, such as skin cancers in humans.

Ozone naturally decays by converting back into normal oxygen (O_2), but the ozone layer is perpetually replenished as ozone forms naturally in the stratosphere. However pollutant

Previous page: This image demonstrates vividly the fact that ice has little buoyancy, so that most of an iceberg remains below the water line. Icebergs float because the density of the ice is lower than that of seawater, but about 7/8 of their mass lies below the surface.

gases, such as CFCs (chlorofluorocarbons), which are used as the propellant in some aerosols and in refrigeration systems, and halons, compounds used in fire extinguishers, speed up the rate of decay, so that now the rate of natural ozone replenishment can't keep up with the rate of decay. The ozone layer is very thin, like a film of oil on water, so the depletion of ozone results in holes appearing, through which ultraviolet radiation can penetrate.

Above each geographical pole there is a vortex of air, caused by wind currents and the rotation of the planet. These vortices become extremely cold, minus 112°F (-80°C), in the absence of sunlight during the winter months, and create the right conditions for stratospheric clouds to form. The presence of clouds encourages the chemical reactions that enable pollutants to deplete the ozone.

Thankfully for humans, the ozone hole is situated over the Antarctic, where few people live, so the health risk to mankind as a whole is not yet that perilous. However, if global pollution levels are allowed to rise, then the ozone hole will increase in size until it may envelop highly populated areas in the temperate region – South America, Australia, Africa. Worse will follow if a similar-sized ozone hole develops over the North Pole, and already a relatively small one has been identified there as well.

The Antarctic ozone hole was first detected in 1985 by the British Antarctic Survey. This followed a prediction, by scientists in the 1970s, that pollutants would have this effect. Governments of first-world countries are now endeavoring to reduce global emissions of ozone-depleting gases, but it is proving difficult to achieve international consensus as some countries are reluctant to change their industrial processes for economic reasons.

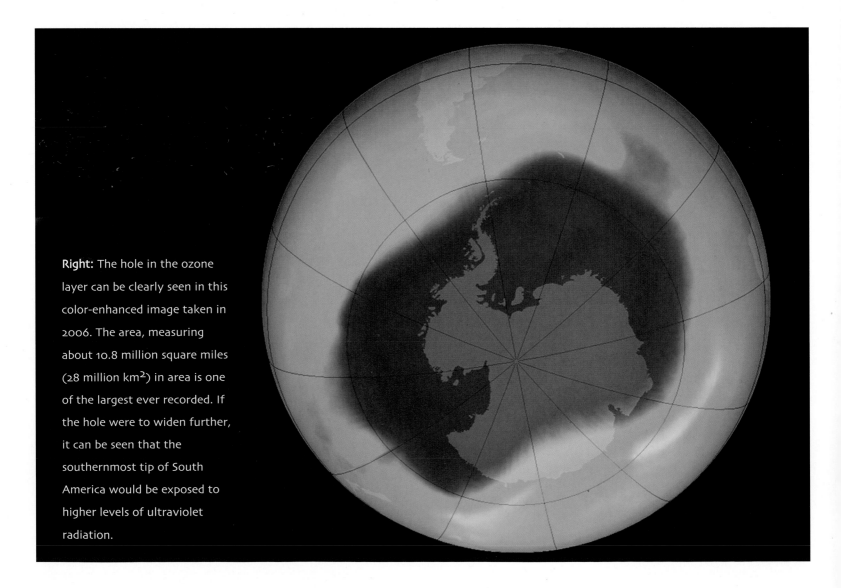

Right: The hole in the ozone layer can be clearly seen in this color-enhanced image taken in 2006. The area, measuring about 10.8 million square miles (28 million km²) in area is one of the largest ever recorded. If the hole were to widen further, it can be seen that the southernmost tip of South America would be exposed to higher levels of ultraviolet radiation.

Right: A party of scientists navigate their way through ice-laden waters. The presence of people in photographs of polar landscapes helps to provide some idea of scale. With the boats in the foreground, it is possible to estimate that the ice cliffs in the background must be several hundreds of feet high.

Below: Two ice sheets have been pushed together, so that their edges have rucked up to form a mini mountain of ice. On a small scale, this mimics what happens when two tectonic plates collide and mountains are formed.

GLOBAL WARMING

The issue of atmospheric pollution is related to another potentially serious and contentious problem – the phenomenon known as 'global warming.' Scientists are divided in their opinions about whether the Earth is warming as part of a natural interglacial phase or because pollutant gases are insulating the Earth to cause a 'greenhouse effect' whereby heat is trapped by carbon dioxide in the atmosphere, which causes the planet to warm. Of course, it is quite likely that both factors are involved simultaneously. There also exists a third possibility that the Earth isn't warming at all on a long-term basis, but merely going through a brief warm spell. Just as it has also been through brief cold spells in recent history.

Whatever the truth of the matter, scientists are now expressing serious concern about the issue of global warming because of the potentially catastrophic effects it will have on the world. Antarctica and Greenland store vast amounts of water in the form of ice sheets, several miles thick. Were the ice to melt, it would raise the level of the oceans by tens of feet and have a profound effect on the coastlines of every landmass. Large areas of land would be lost to the sea and millions of people would be

Above: This pack ice has broken up in an intriguing geometric pattern. Scientists are concerned that global warming may be speeding up the rate at which the Antarctic ice is melting.

Right: Adélie penguins gathering on an ice floe. Adélies are very adept at moving around on an icy surface, and often sled down inclines on their bellies. They nest along the shores of most of Antarctica.

displaced. In 2005 scientists from the British Antarctic Survey reported that global warming appeared to be melting the ice cap faster than had previously been estimated and they warned that Antarctica could become a 'giant awakened.'

In addition to the danger of rising sea levels, global warming would radically change the climatic make-up of the entire planet and the changes would happen far too quickly for many species to adapt to the new conditions by evolutionary means. The ecology of the planet would be put into a tailspin and there would be far-reaching consequences for all plants and animals on the globe.

In short, it might sound the death knell for humanity altogether by catalysing one of the great extinctions that have punctuated the evolution of life on Earth over billions of years. What is most worrying is that scientists have calculated that an average rise in temperate of only a few degrees could tip the balance and lead to a runaway situation in which temperature rise becomes self-sustaining.

DEADLY BROTHER AND SISTER

El Niño (the little boy) and La Niña (the little girl) are ocean currents that periodically have a profound effect on the Antarctic and subantarctic environment.

Above the tropic of Capricorn trade winds called the Easterlies typically circulate the globe in a westward direction. They warm the surfaces of the Atlantic and Pacific oceans and push the warmed water to the west. After a while the sea level rises to the west and falls to the east due to the difference in water density. Eventually, when the winds subside, a critical point is reached and the warm water suddenly flows eastward in a counter-current over the top of the cold water, which flows westward beneath. In the Atlantic this is known as El Niño and in the Pacific it is La Niña. The name was coined by South American fishermen who observed that the phenomenon usually occurred around Christmas time when the birth of the Christ child – El Niño in Spanish – is celebrated.

The effect that these currents have is to kill off plankton in the ocean, as the warm water lacks sufficient nutrition and oxygen to sustain them. The knock-on effect is that the balance of the food chain is severely disrupted, leading to the deaths of many animals higher up the chain, from krill to fish and from birds to mammals.

The Antarctic is affected because the currents are deflected southward by the western coasts of Africa and South America. So the Southern Ocean becomes a vortex of relatively barren water,

where normal fecundity falls off for a time until the natural balance is once again restored.

El Niño occurs about once every two to five years, while La Niña happens roughly half as frequently. When one happens in

the absence of the other then the effect on the Antarctic is not so pronounced, but the combined effect of both can be catastrophic, causing entire penguin colonies to fail to rear their young through lack of food, for example.

Above: Scientists from the British Antarctic Survey are joined by inquisitive crabeater seals beneath the ice at Signy Island. Their scientific researches include projects to monitor the extent and duration of the sea ice cover.

THE METEORITE HARVEST

The Earth is constantly being showered with cosmic debris, which we know as meteors. Most meteors vaporize when they hit the planet's atmosphere, but some are big enough for their cores to survive the fiery journey through the atmosphere and land on Earth. These cores are what we call meteorites. Thousands of meteorites land on Earth every day, but most either fall into the oceans or settle in places on land where they cannot be easily found or identified.

This is where Antarctica comes in useful. It is a vast area of whiteness, so that meteorites stand out clearly on the surface. All scientists have to do is systematically search for them and collect them. It's rather like using an enormous white sheet to collect moths. The reason why scientists are so interested in meteorites is that they originate from the time of the formation of the Solar System and have remained chemically unaltered since that time. This means that analysis of meteorites can tell cosmologists a great deal about how the Solar System, the Milky Way galaxy, and the universe itself all came into being.

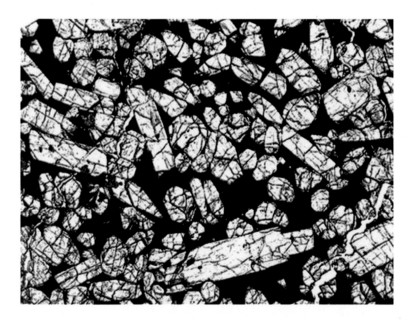

Above: This is a polished wafer of meteorite as viewed under a microscope, showing its crystalline structure. Meteorites are ancient mineral fragments that fall to Earth from space and they provide scientists with the oldest materials of the Solar System for research.

Right: When geologists conduct fieldwork on Antarctica, they have to be mindful that they are working in a potentially life-threatening environment. Clothing, shelter, and communication equipment have to be able to withstand the bitter cold.

FROZEN IN TIME

Because much of the ice on Antarctica never thaws, any new snow that falls is continually being compressed into new layers of ice on top. So the deeper down into the ice you penetrate, the older is the ice you sample. This means that the layers of ice themselves can provide scientists with chemical information about the past. The ice itself is not just frozen water, but contains

other chemicals present in the atmosphere when the water vapor turned to snow and then fell on Antarctica. There are also particulate pollutants, such as dust, pollen grains, and micro-organisms that were present in the air at the time. In addition, the ice contains ancient bubbles. These are places where air between the snow flakes was compressed and entombed by the ice. Like the ice, these bubbles can be chemically analysed, to see what gases are present in them and in what ratios.

Scientists are therefore able to collect and collate very useful data about the Earth in historic and prehistoric times, in much the same way that they do by studying the layers of deposition in lakes and marshes. The method is known as core sampling. A cylindrical tool is bored down into the substrate – whether it be ice, mud, or rock – and then drawn back up with a rod-shaped sample at its core. The sample comprises layers rather like a stack of coins, so that each one represents a different year, season, or event in the past.

Previous pages: In this setting it seems remarkable that penguins can eke out a living from the Antarctic. But the species that live here – emperors, kings, macaronis, Adélies, gentoos, and chinstraps – are able to incubate their eggs and bring up their young in such forbidding terrain.

Above: A group of scientists study the structure within an iceberg. The darker translucent veins are solid ice, where snow has melted and then refrozen. The surrounding substance is compacted snow, which maintains its crystalline structure, with the result that it is opaque and reflects more light.

Right: This is a view of Mount Michael, an active volcano on Saunders Island, one of the South Sandwich Island archipelago. The volcano is known to have erupted explosively in 1819 while the Russian explorer, Fabian Gottlieb von Bellingshausen, was charting the area. Now it sleeps restlessly and vapors are frequently seen rising from its summit crater.

THE EXPLORATION OF THE ANTARCTIC

The first people known to have crossed the Antarctic Circle were the British seafarer and explorer Captain James Cook (1728–79) and his crews aboard the *Resolution* and *Adventure*. The expedition left England in 1772 in search of the 'Terra Australis' or the Southern Continent. They returned in 1775 having only seen the pack ice surrounding Antarctica.

The first official sighting of Antarctica proper came 45 years later in 1820, by Russian explorer Fabian Gottlieb von Bellingshausen (1778–1852) aboard the *Vostok*. He came within 20 miles (32km) of shore.

The first person to claim that he had set foot on Antarctica was an American seal hunter named Captain John Davis in 1821, although it isn't known whether the landfall was actually made on the mainland or an offshore island, due to the presence of ice.

Over the next 20 years a number of explorers investigated and mapped the coastline of Antarctica. They included James Weddell (1787–1834), Jules Dumont d'Urville (1790–1842), Charles Wilkes (1798–1877), and James Clark Ross (1800–62).

Between 1843 and 1897 Antarctica was only visited by sealers and whalers. Then, from 1898 and 1900, groups of Belgian, Norwegian, and British explorers arrived and they managed to survive for long periods on the coast. The turn of the 20th century heralded a new phase in Antarctic exploration – the push

to discover the interior and reach the geographical and magnetic South Poles.

The Anglo-Irish explorer Ernest Shackleton (1874–1922) commanded the first expedition to reach the magnetic South Pole in early 1909. The Norwegian Roald Amundsen (1872–1928) led his triumphant expedition to the geographical South Pole in late 1911. Other early interior expeditions were led by Robert Scott (1868–1912) and Douglas Mawson (1882–1958). Since the 1930s various self-styled 'explorers' have traversed the continent in all manner of ways, sometimes just for the sheer challenge, it would seem.

In 1959 the International Antarctic Treaty was signed by 12 countries in agreement that Antarctica should remain protected from territorial claims. The area between the geographical South Pole and latitude 60 degrees south was designated a zone for

Right: Antarctica has proved to be quite a draw to ecotourists over recent years. Advances in technology have made it relatively comfortable and convenient for holiday makers of a more adventurous frame of mind to visit the continent for short stays during the summer months.

peaceful purposes and scientific research only. In 1991 an updated treaty imposed a 50-year ban on mineral exploitation of the continent, and in 1994 the International Whaling Commission set up the Antarctic whale sanctuary.

PEOPLE IN ANTARCTICA

There have never been any native human populations living on Antarctica, simply because the environment is too hostile for people to survive without the benefits of advanced technology. Indigenous peoples have managed to survive in the Arctic only because they are able to migrate to warmer areas when conditions demand it.

The first people to stay on Antarctica for any length of time were a mix of Belgian, Norwegian, and British explorers who survived the 1898–99 winter there. Since then technology has advanced so much that people are now able to live comfortably in ice stations more or less as they would elsewhere in the world. Even so, they are largely dependant on external support from operations centers situated outside the Antarctic region. Telecommunications, ocean vessels, and aircraft form vital links to the outside world. In many respects ice stations are just as remote as space stations. This is especially true in the depth of

Above: A dog team of Scott's Antarctic expedition rest by an iceberg. The dogs, like many of the items Scott brought with him, proved unsuitable to the task of exploration around the South Pole.

Left: The famous photograph of Robert Scott and his expedition party looking dejected in 1912 having been beaten to the South Pole by Roald Amundsen. Scott wrote 'Great God! This is an awful place and terrible enough for us to have laboured to it without the reward of priority.'

winter, when there is virtually no daylight and the weather is so severe that physical contact is made impossible.

The human 'population' of Antarctica is always in flux because scientists come and go. Around 2500 endure the winter, but numbers are bolstered significantly in the summer, when family, friends, and tourists visit. These can number 7000–9000 over a season.

It is worth noting that the earliest known account of people having visited Antarctica was preserved in the oral history of the Cook Islands in the South Pacific. According to legend a chief of Rarotonga, Ui-te-Rangiora, made a voyage in a double-hulled

Above: In the days of early Antarctic exploration, habitations were made from timber, as it was the easiest material to transport. This photograph shows the interior of a wooden hut used by Ernest Shackleton and his men. The cast iron range provided the welcome comfort of cooked food and heating.

canoe named *Te-Ivi-o-Atea* in the mid-7th century. When Europeans first visited Rarotonga in 1814, they were told tales of the frozen ocean to the south.

Left: In 1916 Ernest Shackleton's ship *Endurance* was trapped in the ice and he and his crew eventually escaped to Elephant Island in the South Shetland Islands. From there, Shackleton and a few men left by whale boat to journey to South Georgia Island to seek help. This photograph shows tourists exploring the beach on Elephant Island from which Shackleton set sail on his incredible 800-mile (1300km) voyage (inset photograph).

Above: An expedition party climbs Devil's Peak on Coronation Island, which is the largest of the South Orkney Islands. Beneath the climbers other small islands can be seen encircled by a frozen sea of pack ice.

Right: This is the entrance to the Amundsen-Scott South Pole Station. The entrance to the geodesic dome was at the surface level of the icecap when it was first erected in the 1970s but the ice has built up around it in the succeeding years.

Above: Ships like this often rely on icebreakers for safe passage through pack ice and ice floes. Icebreakers are built with reinforced bows that plow a path through the ice and push it aside to leave a navigable route, which other ships can use until weather conditions cause the sea to freeze again.

Following pages: Scenes like this lend the Antarctic landscape a mesmerizing beauty, which makes it easy to understand why adventurers are drawn to the continent. Somehow, the very bleakness and inhospitableness of the place acts like a magnet which pulls them inexorably toward the ultimate challenge.

THE WHALING INDUSTRY

When one thinks of Antarctica the first industry that generally comes to mind is whaling, as the Southern Ocean is home to many of the great whale species. In 1994 Antarctica was declared a sanctuary as a measure to ensure that whales had somewhere to escape the harpoons of whaling ships. Even so, the Japanese have continued to cull large numbers of whales, such as minke, fin, and humpback, within the designated area. The Japanese authorities claim that the whales are killed for scientific research purposes, although the meat is sold for human consumption. They claim that the meat sales subsidize the cost of research and the construction of the whaling ships, and so manage to get away with whaling in the name of science. Several hundred whales are killed by the Japanese each year. Most conservation groups condemn the whaling as inhumane and unnecessary, and argue that any scientific objectives can be met through non-lethal research methods.

Iceland and Norway are the only other countries to practice whaling on a significant scale, although most of their harpooning is done in the Arctic and north Atlantic oceans, rather than the Southern Ocean. They are honest enough, however, to admit that it is done for commercial reasons, albeit under the guise of its being necessary to preserve their cultural traditions.

The heyday of whaling was during a period spanning the 19th and 20th centuries. Unimaginable numbers of whales were slaughtered in the pursuit of their waxes and oils which were used in other industries. It wasn't until the 1920s that fractional distillation of petroleum saw an end to whaling on an industrial scale. Happily, it became more convenient and less expensive to manufacture waxes and oils from crude oil, and whaling declined as a result.

Right: In the Antarctic organic debris can remain intact for long periods because conditions are too cold and dry for the natural processes of decay to do their work rapidly. These are the vertebrae and ribs of a fin whale lying on a rocky shore in Port Lockroy, Antarctic Peninsula. Winter storms had scattered the bones but scientists from a nearby research station restored the shape of the skeleton. It was probably slaughtered by whalers a century ago.

LIFE IN THE SEA

All of the fully aquatic marine mammals of the Antarctic are cetaceans – either dolphins, porpoises, or whales. The cetaceans are divided into two suborders: the toothed whales, which includes dolphins and porpoises, and the baleen whales.

Sailors in bygone days understood little of taxonomy. They used to classify the sea creatures they saw according to the visual evidence. Consequently they thought of cetaceans as fish. It wasn't until the Swedish botanist and zoologist Carolus Linnaeus (1707–78) devised a uniform system for naming and classifying all living things that the scientific world realized that they were in fact mammals that had adapted to a marine lifestyle.

Of course, there are fundamental differences between cetaceans and fish. Cetaceans are warm-blooded animals that breathe air and give birth to live young. Fish are cold-blooded animals that breathe by means of gills and produce young from eggs. In addition, fish possess scales while cetaceans do not. There are plenty of anatomical differences too, simply because fish and mammals occupy separate places on the evolutionary tree. Fish are the more primitive group, with amphibians and reptiles in between them and the mammals.

The toothed whales come in a range of sizes to suit specializations in hunting different prey. They eat all kinds of fish as well squid and krill. Some will also kill and eat other mammals and birds, or even resort to eating carrion. They are called 'toothed whales' because they have teeth set in their jaws, in contrast to the baleen whales, which do not.

The baleen whales are more specialized in their feeding habits. They have become filter feeders rather than hunters. They also eat fish, squid, and krill, but mainly consume vast amounts of plankton. This is done by sieving the water through bristle-covered plates called baleen. All of the organisms present in a mouthful of water get filtered out and then swallowed wholesale.

TOOTHED WHALES

The smallest of the toothed whales are the dolphins and porpoises. They are the equivalent of the foxes and wolves of the terrestrial world. They are fast and agile, able to pursue and hunt down fast-moving quarry. They also are gregarious animals that live in extended family groups.

In the Antarctic there are very few species of dolphin and porpoise. This is because they tend to be shallow feeders in temperate waters, preferring the coastal areas of South America, Africa, and Australasia.

The only species that crosses the Antarctic Convergence is the hourglass dolphin (*Lagenorhynchus cruciger*). It looks superficially

Previous page: Humpback whales have a characteristic way of blowing or spouting when they come to the surface to fill their lungs with air. There is always a vertical puff of fine spray or mist which looks rather like a fountain. Other whales blow in differing ways, depending on the species.

Right: This is a dolphin known as the southern rightwhale dolphin. It is so called because it resembles the rightwhale as it too lacks a dorsal fin. Apart from that single detail, however, it is quite dissimilar. Its size is only a fraction of that of the whale, which also lacks the dolphin's two-tone coloring.

like a killer whale as it is pied in color, although it is only about 6ft (1.8m) in length. Its name alludes to sets of paired white markings on its sides which are hourglass or egg-timer in shape. Little is known of the hourglass dolphin's lifestyle, except that it frequents cold waters and is typically sighted far out to sea.

There is also an unusual dolphin species known as the southern rightwhale dolphin *(Lissodelphis peronii)*. It is a small animal with a black back and white belly. This species lacks a dorsal fin and looks much like a large penguin when swimming at the surface. It is an offshore species found in the northern waters of the Southern Ocean.

The spectacled porpoise *(Australophocaena dioptrica)* is also a Southern Ocean species and it too remains outside the Antarctic Convergence zone, frequenting the coastal waters of subantarctic islands and archipelagos. This species is black above and white below, with a clearly contrasting boundary line running down each side of the body. Its name alludes to spectacle-like marking around the eyes – each eye is set in a patch of black, ringed by a white circle. This species has a very rounded dorsal fin, while the hourglass dolphin's is distinctly keel-shaped. Both species seem to be distributed right around the polar region.

The medium-sized toothed whales comprise the beaked whales and the pilot whales. The beaked whales are an odd bunch of cetaceans. They specialize in feeding on squid deep down in ocean trenches. As a result isolated populations have evolved into different species, so that there are some 20 currently known to science. Their dentition is unusual in that the number of teeth has been greatly reduced to just two or four on the lower mandible only. They serve to grasp the bodies of their prey, which are then swallowed whole.

Arnoux's beaked whale *(Berardius arnuxii)* is around 30ft (9m) long and gun-metal gray all over. It has been recorded many times by sea traffic passing between Antarctica and ports in Australasia and South America, which suggests that it has a circumpolar range throughout the Southern Ocean. It is identifiable by its very small and back-set dorsal fin. If the head is seen, the thin snout with visible front teeth that glisten white are also distinctive.

The southern bottlenose whale *(Hyperoodon planifrons)* is another beaked whale of similar appearance and range. It varies in color greatly, from black to gray and brown to beige. It has a more rounded forehead and shorter snout, which is reminiscent of a dolphin.

The pilot whales of the Antarctic region are the long-finned pilot whale *(Globicephala melas)* and the killer whale *(Orcinus orca)*. They are very different in terms of lifestyle and behavior.

The long-finned pilot whale is a fisherman by nature, taking both fish and squid in its catch. With its bulbous forehead, it is not dissimilar to the sperm whale in general appearance, although it is much smaller. It has evolved to dive deep after its prey. It has a large keel-shaped dorsal fin, but this tends to droop out of water as though it were a rubber inflatable in need of topping up with some air.

The killer whale is an efficient and intelligent hunter, capable of solitary or pack behavior like the lion in the terrestrial world. It will take fish and squid too, but it has a penchant for seals and seabirds. It will also take the calves of other cetaceans when an opportunity arises. The killer whale is slightly larger than its pilot whale cousin, at about 30ft (9m) in length. It is readily recognized at sea by its very tall and erect dorsal fin, which has a triangular profile not unlike that of a large shark.

The pelvic fins of the pilot whale are long, but they are strictly for aquatic use. Indeed, this species is one of those most commonly found stranded on beaches. On the other hand, the killer whale has large, paddle-like pelvic fins, which serve almost as limbs as well as flippers. This makes it possible for the animal to charge into the shallows near beaches in pursuit of seals and penguins. Having grabbed the prey in its mouth, it then writhes its body back into the water, using its pelvic fins to help it on its way.

The pilot whale is almost entirely blue-black in color, while the killer whale sports a piebald coloring. The only species it might be confused with is the hourglass dolphin, although it is much larger as an adult.

The term 'large toothed whale' is synonymous with the sperm whale *(Physeter macrocephalus)* – there are no others. The massive head of the sperm whale contains something known as the spermaceti organ. It comprises two cavities – the spermaceti sac above and the junk below. The cavities are triangular in profile and fit together to form a rectangle. They contain networks of tubes filled with a waxy oil, known as spermaceti, which is very sensitive to ultrasonic vibrations. The density of the spermaceti varies so that the whale can detect a range of sonar pitches.

Right: Pilot and killer whales, known collectively as 'blackfish,' fall somewhere between dolphins and sperm whales in terms of their size. Here a pair of adult pilot whales are seen with a calf. Like all mammals, young whales are fed initially on milk before being weaned onto solid food.

It would seem that the spermaceti organ is primarily a communication device, rather like an enormously overdeveloped inner ear, able to interpret the faint calls of other sperm whales many miles away, but which is also able to tune complex sonic replies with enough amplitude to travel equal distances. It may also serve a secondary role as a depth gauge and orientation device while diving for the giant squid that make up the whale's diet.

From a front-on perspective the head of the sperm whale is surprisingly asymmetrical, with its blowhole set to the animal's left. This is because the two cavities overlap one another to form a lopsided shape. Looking at the skull, it appears that the animal has a long thin snout, because the spermaceti organ sits on top.

The lower jaw has rows of equally spaced teeth, while the upper jaw is flat and smooth. This arrangement enables the whale to seize its prey and hold it firm until its death throes are over. Grip on the squid can then be released and the prey swallowed whole.

Above: Here a killer whale is breaching the surface at speed, so that virtually the whole of its body is clear of the surface. The fact that such a large animal can do this is testament to the immense power it has at its disposal. This power translates into impressive speed and momentum while hunting underwater.

Following pages: This is a sight that never fails to excite whale watchers. It is the classic pose of a humpback whale going into a dive by raising its tail flukes into the air. The ventral (under) surfaces of the flukes bear distinctive white markings, from which zoologists can tell individuals apart.

BALEEN WHALES

The baleen whales of the Antarctic region are from the rorqual family. They include the blue whale *(Balaenoptera musculus)* and its smaller cousins, the fin whale *(B. physalis)*, minke whale *(B. acutorostrata)*, and the sei whale *(B. borealis)*. They are all very streamlined and graceful whales, designed for trawling the oceans for their bounty of small animals, such as plankton and krill. Their throats are pleated to allow them to take enormous gulps of water and then close their mouths. The water is forced out through baleen plates, situated where the teeth would normally be in the upper jaw, so that the food animals are left stranded inside the mouth. It is then a simple matter for the whales to mold the food into boluses with their tongues, ready for swallowing.

The rorquals are migratory species, as they need to take advantage of seasonal gluts in the availability of food. Consequently the same species are seen in both the Arctic and Antarctic, but at different times of the year, six months apart.

The blue whale is the largest rorqual species at some 98ft (30m), while the minke is the smallest at about 33ft (10m). The

Above: All baleen whales, such as this humpback whale, have two blow holes, while all toothed whales have just one. Blow holes are nostrils that have migrated to the upper surface of the snout.

others vary in size. All have small, keel-shaped dorsal fins and very flat backs.

The humpback whale *(Megaptera novaeangliae)* is another worldwide migratory species in the same family as the rorquals. It lacks the elegance of its cousins though. It has a dumpy body with disproportionately long pelvic fins, which are covered in knobs and callosities as is the snout. It is a commonly sighted whale, because it displays close to shore by breaching the surface and slapping its large flippers on the surface of the water.

Humpbacks are also classic lobtailers, making it easy to identify them as they raise their tails high into the air before descending again under the water. Their tails have a distinctive notch between the flukes, which are counter-curved in shape with scalloped or serrated edges.

ANTARCTIC SEALS

In many respects the pinnipeds (seals and sea lions) can be viewed as the amphibious stage that the whales and dolphins must have passed through during their transition many millions of years ago from terrestrial to marine lifestyles. They are not related, but they have similar characteristics, especially as both are descended from carnivorous antecedents.

The pinnipeds seem to have evolved from a bear-like or dog-like ancestor around 30 million years ago. There are three families in the order: the eared seals, such as sea lions and fur seals, the earless or true seals, and a family that contains just one species, the walrus of the Arctic.

In the Antarctic half a dozen species of pinniped are found. Five are true seals and one is an eared seal. A key difference between the two types is seen in their flippers. True seals typically have small flippers attached laterally to the body. They only use them for steering in water, as they use their hind limbs for propulsion. This means that their flippers are of little or no use on land or ice, so the animals have to move around by means of caterpillar-like undulations of the body.

Eared seals, on the other hand, have more robust flippers, which are positioned beneath the body. They use their flippers both for propulsion and for steering in water. In addition, their flippers can be used as limbs on land or ice, enabling the animals to lift their bodies and walk, or rather lollop, along. They also have small external ears, while true seals only have orifices.

Like whales and penguins, pinnipeds have a layer of fat beneath their skins for the purpose of insulation and as a food reserve. Inevitably, they too have been exploited by man for their blubber, as well as fur and other products.

In the Southern Ocean the Antarctic fur seal *(Arctocephalus gazella)* and southern elephant seal *(Mirounga leonina)* were the species particularly hard hit by the sealing industry, because they congregated in large herds during the breeding season. Commercial exploitation of the animals took over from native harvesting in the late 18th century and its heyday was in the early 19th century during the Industrial Revolution, when whale, seal, and penguin oils were in great demand as fuels for lighting, lubricants for machinery, and ingredients in manufacturing processes.

Below: Male southern elephant seals are considerably larger than the females. This phenomenon is known as sexual dimorphism. Here two males are seen sparring on South Georgia Island.

Left: This photograph clearly demonstrates the difference between true seals and eared seals, such as this Antarctic fur seal. Its ability to clamber onto such ragged rocks is due to the fact that it has leg-like flippers that enable it to walk. True seals can only haul themselves in ungainly fashion onto flat surfaces.

Opposite: Weddell seals are true seals. Although they are elegant swimmers and efficient hunters, on land they are fat blobs barely able to hoist themselves out of the water. They do so by muscular undulations of the body, not dissimilar to the way caterpillars walk along leaves.

The animals were clubbed to death before being skinned and then having their blubber stripped away. The blubber was boiled down to extract valuable oil, which was barrelled up for transportation back to civilization. The furs were washed in salt water and also packed into barrels as rawhide. The sealing industry ultimately petered out, just as whaling and penguining did, in the first half of the 20th century. Petroleum oils became readily available and relatively inexpensive, which knocked the bottom out of the market for animal oils. In addition, public opinion and an increased awareness of the importance of conservation led to vocal criticism of the cruelty of the industry.

The Antarctic fur seal has breeding colonies on various islands close to the peninsula as well as various other subantarctic islands and archipelagos. They feed primarily on fish, squid, and krill, but will also take penguins if they get a chance. The male is about the length of a grown man, although a good deal heavier. The female is smaller. As their name suggests, fur seals have a thick coat, which grows into a mane around the forequarters of the males. It is the only eared seal species of the region.

The southern elephant seal has a similar distribution to the fur seal. It is a much larger animal though. Males on average grow to around 14ft (4.5m) and females to 10ft (3m) in length. Their name refers to their sheer 'elephantine' size and the fact that they have elephant-like skin. In addition, male elephant seals have a trunk-like proboscis, which they inflate with air as a display of machismo to stake their claim over the right to mate with females. The dominant bulls keep harems of cows and defend them against other male suitors. They are rather clumsy when it comes to paternal care, however, often inadvertently crushing their own calves to death while fighting their battles.

The crabeater seal *(Lobodon carcinophagus)* has the distinction of being the most numerous of the large wild mammals on Earth. Estimates of its population are put at 12–15 million. They are adapted to life on or near the pack ice of Antarctica and can be found around the entire coastline of the continent. They are seldom found in groups larger than four or five in number, but they are common animals with a large and even distribution.

Curiously, crabeater seals don't include crabs in their diet. The only crustaceans they eat are krill, which are more like shrimps than crabs. Indeed, they even have serrated teeth that enable them to sieve krill from the seawater. Strictly speaking, most crabeater seals never come to land, because permanent

glacierization exists over most of their range. When they pup they often travel considerable distances over the pack ice so that their young are safe from the attentions of predatory leopard seals and the risk of the summer thaw landing them in the ocean. They have been known to move more than 50 miles (80km) from the ice edge.

Their offspring are fed on an extremely rich milk with high-fat content, which sees them develop rapidly. At only five or six weeks old they are ready to enter the water for the first time. Juveniles and adults tend always to remain close to the pack ice, so they migrate north and south with the seasons.

The leopard seal (*Hydrurga leptonyx*) is considerably larger than the crabeater seal, at around 9ft 2in (2.8m) in length. Its name alludes to its spotted coat, but it is also leopard-like in its behavior too. It is a lithe animal, with a reptilian-looking head, and is able to hunt and pursue all manner of prey, including other seals and penguins as well as fish, squid, and krill. It is an all-round predator that counts the killer whale as its only natural foe.

Leopard seals have something of a reputation for being fearless and aggressive. When they attack penguins, they shake the birds so violently that their skins come loose and ruffle up like rolled-down socks. This is a technique to get at the flesh without having to consume mouthfuls of feathers. Like real leopards, these seals are solitary in habits.

The Weddell seal (*Leptonychotes weddelli*) is named after James Weddell (1787–1834) who was the captain of a sealer vessel, the *Jane*, that reached the Weddell sea in 1823. Weddell seals are large animals around 10ft (3m) long and 992lb (450kg) in weight. They live in the pack ice known as fast-ice, so-called because it holds fast and never melts. To maintain their amphibious lifestyle they use chains of breathing holes and haul-out holes. These are created by locating thin pack ice and sawing away at it with their teeth, which are specially adapted for the job. This adaptation enables them to survive in more southerly latitudes than any other mammal.

The final Antarctic species is the Ross seal (*Ommatophoca rossi*), named after James Clark Ross (1800–62), the British naval officer who explored Antarctica between 1839 and 1843. This seal is relatively scarce and little studied by science. It is known to specialize in hunting squid at depth, which is why it has unusually large eyes to absorb as much available light as possible, much as nocturnal terrestrial predators have.

Left: The leopard seal is clearly different from its fish-eating cousins. Its body form is much the same as other true seals, but its head is quite untypical. The enormous gape and dentition that we see here betray the fact that it is a formidable hunter of other marine mammals and penguins.

Following pages: The crabeater seal has multilobed teeth that enable it to sieve the krill that form its staple diet from the seawater. The term crab was once a generic term for crustaceans, which is why the seal came to be called the crabeater and not the 'krilleater' which would be more accurate.

ANTARCTIC BIRDS

There are no terrestrial Antarctic mammals, either on Antarctica itself or its surrounding islands and archipelagos. This is simply because they would need to migrate to avoid the harsh conditions of winter. Consequently the nearest terrestrial mammals are to be found in South America. Similarly, there are no amphibians or reptiles on Antarctica. The conditions in this harshest of environments are simply too extreme for them to survive. The animals that are seen on the Antarctic ice are principally birds – most famously penguins. The fossils of a dozen or so giant penguin species have been found. These birds stood nearly 5ft (about 1.5m) tall and must have weighed around 220lb (100kg), suggesting that they were adapted to a polar environment of unimaginable frigidity.

PENGUINS

Of the 17 recognized types of penguin, just six qualify as truly Antarctic species. That is to say, only six species are found either on the mainland of Antarctica itself or on nearby islands (or both). The other 11 species live on more distant, subantarctic islands or outside the Antarctic region altogether.

The name 'penguin' is borrowed from the great auk, a similar but unrelated bird from the northern hemisphere which originally bore the name before it became extinct. It may have been derived from the Latin 'penna-gigno' meaning 'feather-provider' as great auks were harvested for their down. Alternatively the root may be the Latin 'pinguis' meaning fat and stupid, due to the fact that the birds were rotund and flightless and made little or no attempt to evade capture.

All penguins are flightless, amphibious birds. Their wings have been reduced to flippers, which they use to propel and steer themselves through the water. Losing the power of flight meant that they no longer needed to remain lightweight. This allowed them to increase in size and fatten up. Having a low surface-area-to-mass ratio and plenty of fatty insulation made them well suited to survival in cold environments and enabled them to fill niches that were out of bounds to other birds. The fact that they were unable to fly did not pose a problem, because few predators were able to reach the birds in their remote habitats.

Penguins exhibit a number of characteristics that demonstrate exactly how they have come to cope so well with their surroundings. They have torpedo-shaped bodies that optimize their streamlining so that they move efficiently and easily in water. Their heads are orientated so that their beaks are in line with their bodies too. This helps with streamlining and also allows the birds to look forward and grasp fish while moving at

Previous page: This picture graphically illustrates the bleakness of the habitat in which Antarctic penguins have to survive. Large amounts of body fat help to keep out the cold.

Right: King penguins look similar to emperor penguins, but their plumage is more colorful and contrasting. They are deep water specialists that feed mainly on squid, and they can dive to prodigious depths in pursuit of their prey.

speed in the water. Their tails and feet serve no function in the water, so they are tucked away at the rear to reduce drag, while their flippers are shaped like blades to cut easily through the water.

Penguins are covered in feathers, but they are generally reduced and have the appearance of a coat of fur. This is partly to improve streamlining and partly to provide much needed insulation out of the water. Their plumage has been dubbed the 'diving suit' in contrast with the 'pyjama suit' of downy feathers that the chicks and juveniles have. Even the overall coloring of penguins is indicative of their marine habit. They are counter-shaded, so that they are white below and black above while swimming. This makes it more difficult for predators to spot them from above and below. Penguins also feed in flocks, which predators find visually confusing which makes it harder for them to single out an individual to make a kill.

Out of water penguins are rather clumsy as their aquatic design features make moving around far more awkward on dry land. They only get away with it because they don't have terrestrial predators to worry about. Due to the position of their legs they have to balance in an upright posture, using their feet and tails to stabilize them. To move about they either waddle or hop, although they will often resort to tobogganing on their bellies if there is snow cover. The problem of coming back to land from water is often overcome by the penguins shooting upward out of the water and then landing on their feet. If there is a beach available, then they normally prop themselves up on their feet while in shallow water. Returning to water is done by shallow diving.

When explorers first ventured to the Southern Ocean, they had to rely heavily on finding food and provisions as they went along. Malnutrition could be so dire that sailors actually went mad and died of starvation and disease. It is little surprise that sailors had no qualms about killing and eating any animals that they came across during their travels. Penguin colonies were seen

as bountiful larders of easily accessible fresh meat and eggs. Literally thousands of the birds would be collected in a single visit and preserved by drying or salting the meat. Once the crew was satiated with fresh food and the ship fully victualled, then the voyage could continue.

Apparently penguin meat has a rather fishy flavor and is tough in texture, making it quite unpalatable. However, it was preferable to old stale supplies and was certainly nutritious. The fatty skin of the penguins was flayed and the meat was stewed, roasted, or boiled. The eggs, on the other hand, were regarded a delicacy.

The exploitation of penguin colonies began on a grand scale in the late 16th century and petered out in the late 19th to early 20th centuries. Before that period indigenous peoples had traditionally harvested birds and eggs. Such traditions still continue as a means of scratching out a modest living.

The birds were prized for their fat and skins, as well as the meat. Their feathers are so small and tightly packed that their skins provide a luxuriant silky material that has been used for making clothing, hats, shoes, bags, and purses. In addition, the molted feathers of penguins can be collected and used to stuff pillows and mattresses.

Penguin fat had huge commercial value before the discovery of petroleum fractions, which meant that millions of birds were slaughtered to yield penguin oil. Penguin oil, seal oil, and whale oil were all in great demand for various industrial uses. They were ingredients in the manufacture of products as diverse as soaps, cosmetics, fuels, and medicinal preparations.

A factory on the Macquarie Islands, established in 1891, was the issue that led to a major shift in public opinion about the exploitation of animal resources. Propaganda was spread that the penguins were being boiled alive. It was untrue but it led to organized opposition to the venture. Joseph Hatch, the company owner, assured conservationists that he was harvesting penguins in a sustainable way and that the colonies were actually increasing in size. However, his license was not renewed by the New Zealand government when it expired in 1920. Ironically, it turned out that Hatch had been correct in his assertions when scientists assessed the state of the Macquarie penguin rookeries in the years that followed.

A valuable by-product of penguins is guano – their dried droppings or dung. It is used as a very rich agricultural fertilizer. Large penguin colonies can yield thousands of tons of guano, as it builds up in layers over successive years until it is several feet thick. Even after the introduction of man-made fertilizers, the

guano industry remains viable on a local level, simply because it is a free resource that doesn't cost much to bag-up and transport. Also it does the penguins no harm, as long as harvesting is not conducted during the breeding season.

The plight of penguins entered the public consciousness in the late 19th century, but they did not receive any proper legal protection until the early 20th century. In 1905 the International Ornithological Congress began to urge governments to consider introducing measures to safeguard penguins. South Georgia fully

protected its penguins in 1909 and set the ball rolling for other subantarctic territories – a dozen in all. By 1959 12 nations were ready to sign the Antarctic Treaty, which essentially established Antarctica as a nature reserve or sanctuary and protected a number of penguin species in the process.

The species of penguin that is most amazingly well-adapted for Antarctica has to be the emperor penguin *(Aptenodytes forsteri)*. It looks very similar to the king penguin *(A. patagonicus)* of subantarctic habitats, but was distinguished as a separate

Above: This species is called the chinstrap penguin, for obvious reasons. There are an estimated 18 million chinstrap penguins, making it one of the most numerous species. Chinstrap penguins have been known to breed on ice, but they prefer less icy conditions on the rocky shores of the islands farther north.

species in 1775 by Johann Reinhold Forster (1729–98), a German naturalist onboard the *Resolution*, which was captained by James Cook.

Emperor penguins never leave the waters of the high Antarctic and never truly come to land as they inhabit the pack ice floating on the Southern Ocean. They are the largest penguins, standing about 3ft 9in (1.15m) tall and weighing as much as 84lb (38kg). This is part of their adaptation to the cold as increased bulk and a low surface-area-to-mass ratio helps to conserve body warmth. It also ties them to their environment though, as they cannot cope with warmer conditions.

The life history of emperor penguins is quite astonishing, as they breed at the height of the Antarctic winter, when the continent is shrouded in darkness and temperatures plummet to their lowest. As soon as the single egg is laid, the male takes responsibility for incubating it, while the female heads seaward to fatten herself up. The male holds the egg on his feet where it is securely lodged in place beneath a fold of skin. He huddles together with other males during this period until the time comes for the eggs to hatch. Incubation lasts nearly two months. Despite severe weight loss, the male provides the first meal for the chick with a secretion regurgitated from his crop. He then waits for the female to return.

With the chick ensconced with the female, the male heads off to sea for a much needed feed. The female feeds the chick until the male returns to help with parental duties. Once the chick has developed its 'pajama' suit of down, it huddles together with other chicks in a crèche, enabling both parents to hunt for food.

By the time the juvenile bird is ready to go and fish for itself, Antarctica is enjoying the height of summer. This means that the pack ice has receded to give the young penguin a relatively short walk to the ocean. In addition, the waters are home to a plentiful supply of seasonal food animals. The juvenile bird hitches a ride on an ice floe while it molts into its 'diving' suit. Only then can it enter the water.

Emperor penguins eat 90-95 percent fish. The other 5-10 percent of their diet comprises squid and krill. They can hold

Left: These young emperor penguins have developed their downy 'pajama' suits to fend off the cold. Adults and chicks rely on huddling together in extremely cold winter conditions to conserve warmth and gain some protection from the wind.

their breath for almost 20 minutes, enabling them to make very deep dives between 165ft (50m) and 1870ft (565m).

Both the immature birds and the adults spend the summer months fattening themselves. They frequent the open ocean, but tend to remain within the Antarctic Convergence zone where food is relatively abundant. The adult birds are blue-black on their back and head, with white bellies. They have white lozenge-shaped patches on the sides of their necks that fade from yellow to white. There are an estimated 400,000 individuals living in the Antarctic currently.

The other five Antarctica species fall into two genera – *Pygoscelis* and *Eudyptes*. *Pygoscelis* is home to the chinstrap penguin *(Pygoscelis antarctica)*, Adélie penguin *(P. adeliae)*, and the gentoo penguin *(P. papua)*. These are the truly black and white penguins. That is, they have no additional color to their plumage. All are around 24-37in (60-95cm) tall and weigh about 11lb (5kg). They live gregariously in nesting colonies called rookeries, where they make basic nests just out of pecking range of one another from the materials available to them – pebbles, twigs, feathers, grass, and seaweed.

These three species are distinguished visually mainly by their head markings. The chinstrap penguin, as its name suggests, has a thin strap-like black line running under its white chin, so that it looks like it is wearing a black bonnet. The other two species have black heads, but the gentoo has a white stripe across the top of its head joining eye to eye, while the Adélie does not. Occasionally individuals are seen that have white plumage, but they are not albinos, for they still have pigmented eyes and skin.

The genus *Eudyptes* is home to the rockhopper penguin *(Eudyptes chrysocome)* and the macaroni penguin *(E. chrysolophus)*. They are slightly smaller than the *Pygoscelis* species and sport rather showy, golden-yellow crests on their heads. These penguins are quite difficult to distinguish from one another. They are both black above and white below, with orange bills and feet. The difference is in the detail. The rockhopper has a black central swath to its crest, so that it appears to have yellow eyebrows that droop down behind each eye. The macaroni has bushier 'eyebrows' that join in the middle.

Like emperor penguins, all these birds catch a variety of fish, squid and krill. Where they coexist, it is thought that they dive to different depths and specialize in feeding on different prey to avoid direct competition for food.

The macaroni penguin is reckoned to be the most abundant of all the penguin species. It has an estimated population of at least 24 million. The other species are all regionally common too, numbering in their hundreds of thousands if not millions.

Left: Macaroni penguins waddle across the ice of Candlemas Island on their way to the sea. Macaronis feed on a wide variety of prey, taking krill, fish, and small squid.

Opposite: The gentoo penguin is the third largest of the penguin species, after the emperor and the king. Gentoos have orange bills and a distinctive white stripe across the top of their heads.

Left: Gentoo and chinstrap penguins on an iceberg in South Bay at Trinity Island, near the Antarctic peninsula. Sometimes different species of penguin are observed together and this is because they feel safer in larger mixed groups, just as other birds do, such as waders and songbirds. The various methods of getting around on the ice are in evidence, with the bird at the top left choosing to toboggan on its stomach.

OTHER ANTARCTIC BIRDS

The snowy sheathbill *(Chionis alba)* is a curious looking bird, which appears something like a cross between a pigeon and a gull. Indeed, it is regarded as an anomaly amongst zoologists because it doesn't easily fit into the avian classification, such are its odd combination of features.

Its plumage is entirely white, like a domestic fowl. It has pinkish wattles on its face, surrounding each eye and a horny, yellowish sheath covering a blunt bill with a black tip. It legs are either pinkish or blue-gray and look similar to a gull's, except that the feet are only partially webbed. It has relatively small wings, equipped with carpal spurs. These are deployed during disputes over territory.

Sheathbills are found among colonies of penguins, other seabirds, and marine mammals, where they provide a sort of garbage disposal service. They will scavenge and eat just about any items of food they can find, such as dead chicks and broken eggs. They also readily plunder the food of other species, such as fish, squid, and krill that have been spilled on the ground.

These birds frequent the Antarctic peninsula and archipelagos near to that region. They are always reluctant to fly, which is probably an instinctive behavior to prevent them from being blown out to sea. However, when conditions are right, they fly strongly over open water. They are not averse to hitching rides on passing ships either. They nest on ledges close to their food supply and typically raise one or two chicks, although they often lay three or four eggs, just in case its happens to be a good season.

The south polar skua *(Catharacta maccormicki)* has the distinction of being the most southerly bird. Its entire range is within the Antarctic Circle and it has a circumpolar distribution along the coastline of Antarctica. The bird is gull-like in general form, but its plumage is a warm brown color. Like the sheathbill, these skuas are general scavengers, although they will readily attack seabird colonies to acquire chicks and eggs. They will also intercept other birds on the wing and harass them into dropping food. They are the pirates of the Antarctic skies.

A similar species, the Antarctic skua *(Catharacta antarctica)*, also known as the brown skua, is blackish in color and has a more northerly range, extending from the peninsula to many of the subantarctic islands and archipelagos. There is also a species of gull, the kelp gull *(Larus dominicanus)*, which is very similar in appearance and habits to the greater black-backed gull of the northern hemisphere. It has a similar range to the Antarctic skua.

Above: Skuas, or jaegers, are piratical in their habits. They harry other seabirds into dropping their catch of fish, squid, or krill and then claim the food for themselves. This is the Antarctic skua.

Opposite: In marked contrast to the aggressive skuas, petrels are more genteel in nature. This pristine white bird is aptly named the snow petrel. The plumage acts as camouflage to protect it from predators while it nests on snowy cliff ledges.

Intriguingly both Antarctic and Arctic terns are found on the peninsula. The Antarctic tern *(Sterna vittata)* uses the peninsula and subantarctic islands for breeding during the summer months, and then moves north for the winter. The Arctic tern *(Sterna paradisaea)*, on the other hand, does not breed because it is on vacation, having bred six months before in the Arctic. Both birds are similar in appearance, but the Antarctic tern is seen in its summer plumage while at the same time the Arctic tern is wearing its winter plumage.

Terns feed by shallow diving after small fish and krill. They nest on beaches and dunes close to the seashore. Their eggs and chicks are very effectively camouflaged so that they are difficult to distinguish from the background of sand and pebbles.

The blue-eyed shag *(Phalacrocorax atriceps)* is a typical member of the cormorant family. It breeds in colonies on rocky outcrops. The nest is made of bits of flotsam and jetsam, such as seaweed, driftwood, and feathers, cemented together with guano

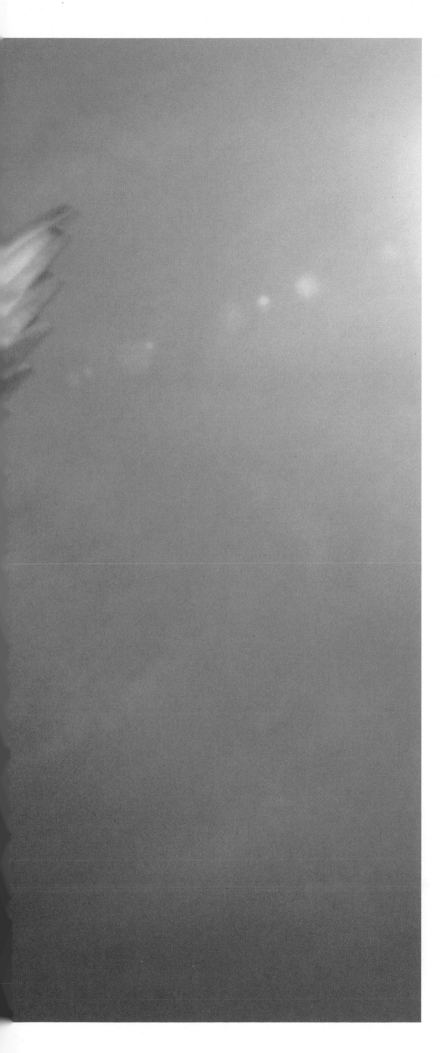

into a mound. The adults and young feed on fish, squid, and krill. The bird is black above and white below from head to tail. It has bright pink fleshy patches on its face, pink feet, and bright blue eye rings, which make it the most colorful of Antarctica's birds.

There are a number of seabirds known collectively as tubenoses, as they have tubular nostrils mounted above their bills. They include albatrosses, petrels, fulmars, prions, shearwaters, storm-petrels, and diving-petrels – all of which are present in Antarctica. They possess special organs in their heads that extract freshwater from seawater. The nasal tubes are where the saline waste is excreted. This adaptation enables tubenoses to survive without the need to drink freshwater or to derive it from non-marine foodstuffs and it has enabled them to conquer oceanic environments where other birds would perish.

The Antarctic petrel *(Thalassoica antarctica)*, the Antarctic prion *(Pachyptila desolata)*, and the snow petrel *(Pagodroma nivea)* are three species that have adapted specifically to the problems of breeding on Antarctica itself. The snow petrel in particular is very much a bird of the snow and ice. It will even dig through snow to expose the ground beneath in order to begin nesting. All the tubenoses feed by picking fish, squid, krill, and planktonic animals from the ocean surface. Many even follow trawlers and whalers to pick up scraps that are present in the wake of the ships.

Wilson's storm petrel *(Oceanites oceanicus)* is one of the most abundant seabirds in the world, and it includes the Southern Ocean in its range. It is a thrush-sized bird with a fluttering flight that specializes in feeding on items of food that are generally too small for other seabirds to bother with. It is undoubtedly a good strategy, since the birds number in their tens of millions. They are called storm petrels because they favor rough conditions that bring planktonic animals to the water's surface.

The only passerine, or perching bird, found in the Antarctic is the South Georgia pipit *(Anthus antarcticus)* which is indigenous to the island of South Georgia. It is very much like the rock and water pipits of Europe, with which it shares its genus name. It is a ground-nesting birds that feeds on insects and other small invertebrates either inland or at the shoreline.

Left: This Arctic tern has a ring around one of its legs. Ringing is an important method used in researching the migratory behavior of birds. This individual would have been ringed while still a juvenile on the nest thousands of miles north in the Arctic.

Below: The kelp gull is very similar to the black and silver backed gulls of the northern hemisphere. It belongs to the same genus and has comparable habits. It is primarily a scavenger, eating just about anything that it can swallow.

Above: Flocks of seabirds on the surface of the water is an indication that a shoal of fish has been discovered. Here a variety of species are competing for food and below the surface other predators may be taking advantage of the opportunity to feed. Albatrosses, gulls, and petrels have all entered the fray.

Right: A wandering albatross in flight over waters off South Georgia Island. The wandering albatross is famed for its ability to remain airborne for weeks on end by riding updrafts. It has the longest wingspan of any bird – up to 11.8ft (3.6m). Pairs of albatrosses produce single chicks once every two years.

POLAR COMPARISONS

ARCTIC

- The first person to reach the geographical North Pole is generally accepted to be the US explorer Robert Peary (1856–1920), who got there on 6 April 1909.
- The Arctic is an ocean surrounded by continents.
- The Arctic sea ice accumulates over several years.

- Land ice is found in limited areas and the largest is the Greenland ice sheet.
- The maximum sea ice extent is 5.8 million square miles (15 million km^2).
- Icebergs are calved from glaciers during the summer months.

- Elevation at the North Pole is 3ft (1m) of sea ice.
- The annual mean temperature at the North Pole is minus 4°F (-20°C).
- The highest point in the Arctic is in Greenland – Gunnbjornsfjeld, 12,139ft (3700m).
- The average thickness of the Arctic icepack is 10-20ft (3-6m).

- Ocean currents bring warm water to the Arctic from the Atlantic and Pacific oceans.
- There are many terrestrial mammals in the Arctic. Most migrate south or hibernate during the winter.
- The Arctic is mostly free of ice and snow in the summer months and supports a variety of plant life.
- The Arctic terrain has trees and plant life which supports a variety of mammals and birds.
- There are indigenous peoples with long cultural histories living on all continents within the Arctic Circle.
- There is a permanent population of 15 million people living in the Arctic region.

- Eight countries own portions of the Arctic: Norway, Sweden, Finland, Russia, the USA, Canada, Denmark (Greenland), and Iceland.
- Resources including oil, gas, minerals, timber, fresh water, fish, and animal products are all commercially exploited in the Arctic.

ANTARCTIC

- The first person to reach the geographical South Pole was Norwegian explorer Roald Amundsen (1872–1928) who set foot there on 14 December 1911.
- The Antarctic is a continent surrounded by an ocean.
- The Antarctic sea ice accumulates annually and more than doubles the size of the continent.
- Over 97 percent of the Antarctic landmass is covered by the unbroken South Polar ice sheet.
- The maximum sea ice extent is 6.9 million square miles (18 million km^2).
- Icebergs are calved from glaciers and shelf ice throughout the year.

- Elevation at the South Pole is 9300ft (2835m) above sea level.
- The annual mean temperature at the South Pole is minus 71°F (-57°C).
- The highest point south of the Antarctic Circle is Vinson Massif on Antarctica, 16,066ft (4897m)
- The average thickness of the Antarctic icepack is 7000ft (2134m).

- Storm winds in the Southern Ocean surrounding Antarctica create a strong ocean current that circles the continent.
- There are no terrestrial mammals on Antarctica.

- The Antarctic interior continent never thaws and therefore cannot sustain plant life.
- The Antarctic does not have a comparable vegetation zone.

- There is no record of indigenous humans ever living on Antarctica.
- There is no permanent human population on Antarctica, only visiting scientists, explorers and other visitors. The population varies from around 2500 in winter to over 30,000 in summer.
- Portions of Antarctica are claimed by many nations, but it is considered to be Internationally owned.

- The natural resources within the Antarctic Circle are not exploited commercially.

POLAR FACTS

ARCTIC

- The largest Arctic ice shelf is the Ward-Hunt Ice Shelf, Ellesmere Island, which has a length of 45 miles (72km) and a width of 12.5 miles (20km).
- The Arctic Ocean is the smallest of the five oceans but is unique because some of it is frozen for most of the year.
- The average depth of the Arctic Ocean is 3406ft (1038m).
- The deepest point in the Arctic Ocean is 17,881ft (5450m) in the Eurasian Basin.
- The Arctic sea ice is an average of 10ft (3m) thick.
- July is the warmest month in the Arctic when the mean temperature rises to 32°F (0°C) but in February the temperature can drop to minus 40°F (-40°C).
- There are estimated to be around 22–26,000 polar bears in the Arctic with 60 percent living in Canadian territory.
- Polar bears have two layers of fur which provide insulation against the bitter Arctic temperatures. When in peak condition they also have a layer of blubber up to 4.5in (11.4cm) thick.
- During hibernation, the body temperature of the Arctic ground squirrel drops from 98.6°F (37°C) to 26.4°F (minus 3.1°C) which is below the freezing point of water and the lowest recorded body temperature of any living mammal.
- Brown bears are usually solitary creatures but there are places in south-eastern Alaska where food is plentiful and there can occasionally be an average of one bear per square mile.
- Caribou are constantly on the move and some migrate more than 3000 miles (4800km) per year. There are almost twice as many caribou living in Alaska than people.
- Coyotes often hunt in packs and can run as fast as 40mph (64km/h) in short bursts making it difficult for prey to escape.
- The territory of an Arctic wolf pack can cover 600–1000 square miles (1554-2600km²).
- Arctic hares can bound at speeds of up to 37mph (60km/h).
- The Arctic tern undertakes the world's longest migration, almost pole to pole. The bird breeds in the Arctic Circle and then migrates during the northern hemisphere winter and travels to the outer edges of the Antarctic ice pack. The annual journey is 21,750 miles (35,000km), nearly equal to flying all the way around the world.

ANTARCTIC

- The world's longest glacier is the Lambert-Fisher glacier, on Antarctica, at 320 miles (515km).
- The world's largest ice shelf is the Ross Ice Shelf of Antarctica, which has a length of 800 miles (1287km) and a width of 500 miles (800km).
- Antarctica is the driest continent on Earth with humidity lower than that of the Sahara Desert.
- Antarctica contains 70 percent of the world's freshwater.
- Antarctica contains 90 percent of the world's ice.
- It is estimated that snow falling at the South Pole takes about 100,000 years to flow to the coast of Antarctica in the form of a glacier before it breaks off into the sea as part of an iceberg.
- Antarctica is 1.4 times larger than the USA, 58 times larger than the UK, larger even than Australia and Europe.
- Less than one percent of Antarctica is ice free.
- Antarctica holds records for having the coldest, windiest and driest places on Earth.
- Mawson scientific station on Antarctica is the windiest place on Earth often recording gusts of up to 154mph (248.4km/h).
- Vostok scientific station on Antarctic recorded the lowest ever temperature: minus 128.6°F (-89.2°C)
- In 1959 12 countries signed the Antarctic Treaty which established it as a region of peace and science, setting territorial claims aside.
- Scientists from the British Antarctic Survey were the first to discover the ozone hole over the Antarctic in the early 1980s.
- Fossils of plants and animals discovered on Antarctica indicate that the continent once had a much warmer climate and was not always situated at the South Pole. It has drifted there over time as a result of tectonic plate movement.
- More than 80 percent of the birds found in the Antarctic region are penguins.
- Penguins can control the flow of blood through their layer of subcutaneous fat. When it is very cold almost no blood passes through the fat but when it is warm the blood flow increases so that the birds can cool off.
- A blue whale gulps 50 tons of water and krill in one mouthful but swallows only the krill.

INDEX

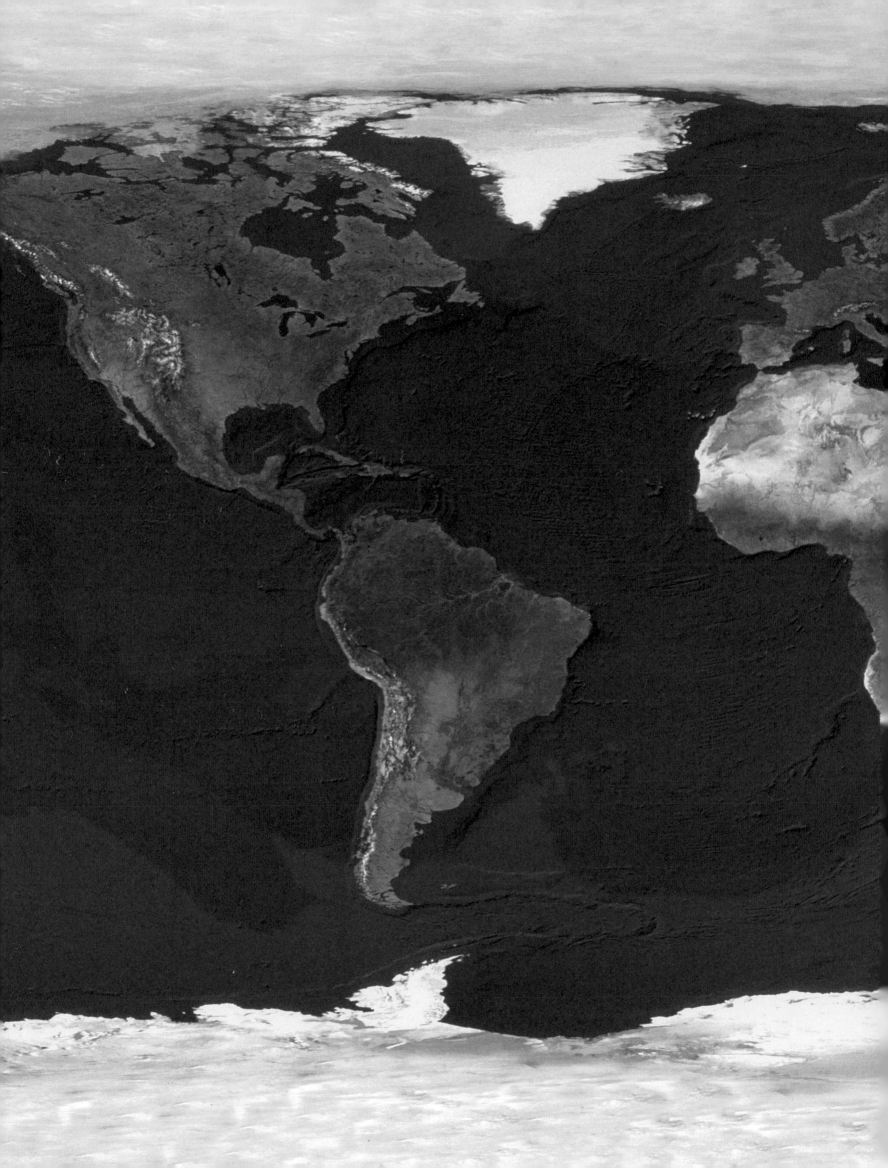